STRAIGHT AT THE TOWER RUSHED THE RED CLOUD, AND HIT
IT A GLANCING BLOW.

Tom Swift and His Airship.

Page 53.

TOM SWIFT AND HIS AIRSHIP

OR

THE STIRRING CRUISE OF THE RED CLOUD

BY
VICTOR APPLETON

AUTHOR OF "TOM SWIFT AND HIS MOTOR-BOAT," "TOM SWIFT AND HIS AIR-
SHIP," "TOM SWIFT AND HIS SUBMARINE BOAT," ETC

FACSIMILE EDITION

1992
BEDFORD, MA
APPLEWOOD BOOKS

The Tom Swift® Adventure Stories were originally published by Grosset & Dunlap. Applewood Books acknowledges the kind permission of Pocket Books, a Division of Simon & Schuster Inc., to reprint these books.

For further information about these editions, please write: Applewood Books, P.O. Box 365, Bedford, MA 01730.

10 9 8 7 6 5 4

Library of Congress Cataloging-in-Publication Data
Appleton, Victor, II.
    Tom Swift and his airship, or, The stirring cruise of the Red Cloud / by Victor Appleton. —Facsimile ed.
        p.   cm.
    Summary: The young inventor builds an airship, makes a trial trip, and experiences a smash-up in midair.
        ISBN 1-55709-177-3
    [1. Airships—Fiction.   2. Adventure and adventurers—Fiction.]   I. Title.   II. Title: Stirring cruise of the Red Cloud.
PZ7.A653A1   1992
[Fic]—dc20   92-29496
                                                CIP
                                                AC

TOM SWIFT AND HIS AIRSHIP

BY

VICTOR APPLETON

AUTHOR OF "TOM SWIFT AND HIS MOTOR-CYCLE," "TOM SWIFT AND HIS
MOTOR-BOAT," "TOM SWIFT AND HIS SUBMARINE BOAT," ETC.

ILLUSTRATED

NEW YORK

GROSSET & DUNLAP

PUBLISHERS

Made in the United States of America

BOOKS BY VICTOR APPLETON

THE TOM SWIFT SERIES

TOM SWIFT AND HIS MOTOR-CYCLE
Or Fun and Adventure on the Road

TOM SWIFT AND HIS MOTOR-BOAT
Or the Rivals of Lake Carlopa

TOM SWIFT AND HIS AIRSHIP
Or the Stirring Cruise of the Red Cloud

TOM SWIFT AND HIS SUBMARINE BOAT
Or Under the Ocean for Sunken Treasure

TOM SWIFT AND HIS ELECTRIC RUNABOUT
Or the Speediest Car on the Road

(Other Volumes in preparation)

12mo. Cloth. Illustrated
postpaid

GROSSET & DUNLAP

PUBLISHERS   NEW YORK

CONTENTS

iii

CONTENTS

TOM SWIFT AND HIS AIRSHIP

CHAPTER I

AN EXPLOSION

"Are you all ready, Tom?"

"All ready, Mr. Sharp," replied a young man, who was stationed near some complicated apparatus, while the questioner, a dark man, with a nervous manner, leaned over a large tank.

"I'm going to turn on the gas now," went on the man. "Look out for yourself. I'm not sure what may happen."

"Neither am I, but I'm ready for it. If it does explode it can't do much damage."

"Oh, I hope it doesn't explode. We've had so much trouble with the airship, I trust nothing goes wrong now."

"Well, turn on the gas, Mr. Sharp," advised Tom Swift. "I'll watch the pressure gauge, and

if it goes too high, I'll warn you, and you can shut
it off."

The man nodded, and, with a small wrench in
his hand, went to one end of the tank. The youth,
looking anxiously at him, turned his gaze now and
then toward a gauge, somewhat like those on
steam boilers, which gauge was attached to an aluminum, cigar-chaped affair, about five feet long.

Presently there was a hissing sound in the
small frame building where the two were conduct·
ing an experiment which meant much to them.
The hissing grew louder.

"Be ready to jump," advised Mr. Sharp.

"I will," answered the lad. "But the pressure
is going up very slowly. Maybe you'd better turn
on more gas."

"I will. Here she goes! Look out now. You
can't tell what is going to happen."

With a sudden hiss, as the powerful gas, under
pressure, passed from the tank, through the pipes,
and into the aluminum container, the hand on the
gauge swept past figure after figure on the dial.

"Shut it off!" cried Tom quickly. "It's coming
too fast! Shut her off!"

The man sprang to obey the command, and,
with nervous fingers, sought to fit the wrench
over the nipple of the controlling valve. Then
his face seemed to turn white with fear.

"I can't move it!" Mr. Sharp yelled. "It's jammed! I can't shut off the gas! Run! Look out! She'll explode!"

Tom Swift, the young inventor, whose acquaintance some of you have previously made, gave one look at the gauge, and seeing that the pressure was steadily mounting, endeavored to reach, and open, a stop-cock, that he might relieve the strain. One trial showed him that the valve there had jammed too, and catching up a roll of blue prints the lad made a dash for the door of the shop. He was not a second behind his companion, and hardly had they passed out of the structure before there was a loud explosion which shook the building, and shattered all the windows in it.

Pieces of wood, bits of metal, and a cloud of sawdust and shavings flew out of the door after the man and the youth, and this was followed by a cloud of yellowish smoke.

"Are you hurt, Tom?" cried Mr. Sharp, as he swung around to look back at the place where the hazardous experiment had been conducted.

"Not a bit! How about you?"

"I'm all right. But it was touch and go! Good thing you had the gauge on, or we'd never have known when to run. Well, we've made another

failure of it," and the man spoke somewhat bit-
terly.

"Never mind, Mr. Sharp," went on Tom Swift.
"I think it will be the last mistake. I see what
the trouble is now; and know how to remedy it.
Come on back, and we'll try it again; that is if
the tank hasn't blown up."

"No, I guess that's all right. It was the aluminum container that went up, and that's so light
it didn't do much damage. But we'd better wait
until some of those fumes escape. They're not
healthy to breathe."

The cloud of yellowish smoke was slowly rolling away, and the man and lad were approaching
the shop, which, in spite of the explosion that had
taken place in it, was still intact, when an aged
man, coming from a handsome house not far off,
called out:

"Tom, is anyone hurt?"

"No, dad. We're all right."

"What happened?"

"Well, we had another explosion. We can't
seem to get the right mixture of the gas, but I
think we've had the last of our bad luck. We're
going to try it again. Up to now the gas has been
too strong, the tank too weak, or else our valve
control is bad."

"Oh dear, Mr. Swift! Do tell them to be careful!" a woman's voice chimed in. "I'm sure something dreadful will happen! This is about the tenth time something has blown up around here, and——"

"It's only the ninth, Mrs. Baggert," interrupted Tom, somewhat indignantly.

"Well, goodness me! Isn't nine almost as bad as ten? There I was, just putting my bread in the oven," went on Mrs. Baggert, the housekeeper, "and I was so startled that I dropped it, and now the dough is all over the kitchen floor. I never saw such a muss."

"I'm sorry," answered the youth, trying not to laugh. "We'll see that it doesn't happen again."

"Yes; that's what you always say," rejoined the motherly-looking woman, who looked after the interests of Mr. Swift's home.

"Well, we mean it this time," retorted the lad. "We see where our mistake was; don't we. Mr. Sharp?"

"I think so," replied the other seriously.

"Come on back, and we'll see what damage was done," proposed Tom. "Maybe we can rig up another container, mix some fresh gas, and make the final experiment this afternoon."

"Now do be careful," cautioned Mr. Swift, the aged inventor, once more. "I'm afraid you two have set too hard a task for yourselves this time."

"No we haven't, dad," answered his son. "You'll see us yet skimming along above the clouds."

"Humph! If you go above the clouds I shan't be very likely to see you. But go slowly, now. Don't blow the place up again."

Mr. Swift went into the house, followed by Mrs. Baggert, who was loudly bewailing the fate of her bread. Tom and Mr. Sharp started toward the shop where they had been working. It was one of several buildings, built for experimental purposes and patent work by Mr. Swift, near his home.

"It didn't do so very much damage," observed Tom, as he peered in through a window, void of all the panes of glass. "We can start right in."

"Hold on! Wait! Don't try it now!" exclaimed Mr. Sharp, who talked in short, snappy sentences, which, however, said all he meant. "The fumes of that gas aren't good to breathe. Wait until they have blown away. It won't be long. It's safer."

He began to cough, choking from the pungent odor, and Tom felt an unpleasant tickling sensation in his throat.

"Take a walk around," advised Mr. Sharp. "I'll be looking over the biue prints. Let's have 'em."

Tom handed over the roll he had grabbed up

when he ran from the shop, just before the explosion took place, and, while his companion spread them out on his knee, as he sat on an upturned barrel, the lad walked toward the rear of the large yard. It was enclosed by a high board fence, with a locked gate, but Tom, undoing the fastenings, stepped out into a broad, green meadow at the rear of his father's property. As he did so he saw three boys running toward him.

"Hello!" exclaimed our hero. "There are Andy Foger, Sam Snedecker and Pete Bailey. I wonder what they're heading this way for?"

On the trio came, increasing their pace as they caught sight of Tom. Andy Foger, a red-haired and squint-eyed lad, a sort of town bully, with a rich and indulgent father, was the first to reach the young inventor.

"How—how many are killed?" panted Andy.

"Shall we go for doctors?" asked Sam.

"Can we see the place?" blurted out Pete, and he had to sit down on the grass, he was so winded.

"Killed? Doctors?" repeated Tom, clearly much puzzled. "What are you fellows driving at, anyhow?"

"Wasn't there a lot of people killed in the explosion we heard?" demanded Andy. in eager tones.

"Not a one," replied Tom.

"There was an explosion!" exclaimed Pete. "We heard it, and you can't fool us!"

"And we saw the smoke," added Snedecker.

"Yes, there was a small explosion," admitted Tom, with a smile, "but no one was killed; or even hurt. We don't have such things happen in our shops."

"Nobody killed?" repeated Andy questioningly, and the disappointment was evident in his tones.

"Nobody hurt?" added Sam, his crony, and he, too, showed his chagrin.

"All our run for nothing," continued Pete, another crony, in disgust.

"What happened?" demanded the red-haired lad, as if he had a right to know. "We were walking along the lake road, and we heard an awful racket. If the police come out here, you'll have to tell what it was, Tom Swift." He spoke defiantly.

"I've no objection to telling you or the police," replied Tom. "There was an explosion. My friend, Mr. Sharp, the balloonist, and I were conducting an experiment with a new kind of gas, and it was too strong, that's all. An aluminum container blew up, but no particular damage was done. I hope you're satisfied."

"Humph! What you making, anyhow?" demanded Andy, and again he spoke as if he had a right to know.

"I don't know that it's any of your business," Tom came back at him sharply, "but, as everyone will soon know, I may as well tell you. We're building an airship."

"An airship?" exclaimed Sam and Pete in one breath.

"An airship?" queried Andy, and there was a sneer in his voice. "Well, I don't think you can do it, Tom Swift! You'll never build an airship; even if you have a balloonist to help you!"

"I won't, en?" and Tom was a trifle nettled at the sneering manner of his rival.

"No, you won't! It takes a smarter fellow than you are to build an airship that will sail. I believe I could beat you at it myself."

"Oh, you think you could?" asked Tom, and this time he had mastered his emotions. He was not going to let Andy Foger make him angry. "Maybe you can beat me at racing, too?" he went on. "If you think so, bring out your *Red Streak* and I'll try the *Arrow* against her. I beat you twice, and I can do it again!"

This unexpected taunt disconcerted Andy. It was the truth, for, more than once had Tom, in his motor-boat, proved more than a match for the squint-eyed bully and his cronies.

"Go back at him, Andy," advised Sam, in low voice. "Don't take any of his guff!"

"I don't intend to," spluttered Andy. "Maybe you did beat me in the races, because my motor wasn't working right," he conceded, "but you can't do it again. Anyhow, that's got nothing to do with an airship. I'll bet you can't make one!"

"I don't bet," replied Tom calmly, "but if you wait a few weeks you'll see me in an airship, and then, if you want to race the *Red Streak* against that, I'll accommodate you. Or, if you want to enter into a competition to build a dirigible balloon or an aeroplane I'm willing."

"Huh! Think you're smart, don't you? Just because you helped save that balloonist from being killed when his balloon caught fire," went on Andy, for want of something better to say. "But you'll never build an airship!"

"Of course he won't!" added Sam and Pete, bound to side with their crony, to whom they were indebted for many automobile and motor-boat rides.

"Just wait," advised Tom, with a tantalizing smile. "Meanwhile, if you want to try the *Red Streak* against the *Arrow*, I'm willing. I have an hour or so to spare."

"Aw, keep still!" muttered Andy, much discomfited, for the defeat of his speedy boat, by a much smaller and less powerful one, was a sore point with him. "You just wait, that's all. I'll get even with you!"

"Look here!" cried Tom, suddenly. "You always say that whenever I get the best of you. I'm sick of hearing it. I consider that a threat, and I don't like it. If you don't look out, Andy Foger, you'll have trouble with me, and at no very distant date!"

Tom, with flashing eyes, and clenched fists, took a step forward. Andy shrank back.

"Don't be afraid of him," advised Sam. "We'll stand by you, Andy."

"I ain't afraid," muttered the red-haired lad, but it was noticed that he shuffled off. " You just wait, I'll fix you," he added to Tom. The bully was plainly in a rage.

The young inventor was about to reply, and, possibly would have made a more substantial rejoinder to Andy than mere words, when the gate opened, and Mr. Sharp stepped out.

"The fumes have all cleared away, Tom," he said. "We can go in the shop, now."

Without further notice of Andy Foger, Tom Swift turned aside, and followed the aeronaut into the enclosed yard.

CHAPTER II

NED SEES MYSTERIOUS MEN

"Who were those fellows?" asked the balloon-ist, of his companion.

"Oh, some chaps who think we'll never build our airship, Mr. Sharp. Andy Foger, and his crowd."

"Well, we'll show them whether we will or not," rejoined the man. "I've just thought of one point where we made a mistake. Your father suggested it to me. We need a needle valve in the gas tank. Then we can control the flow of vapor better."

"Of course!" cried Tom. "Why didn't I think of that? Let's try it." And the pair hurried into the machine shop, eager to make another test, which they hoped would be more successful.

The young inventor, for Tom Swift was en-titled to that title, having patented several ma-chines, lived with his father, Barton Swift, on the outskirts of the small town of Shopton, in

New York State. Mr. Swift was quite wealthy, having amassed a considerable fortune from several of his patents, as he was also an inventor. Tom's mother had been dead since he was a small child, and Mrs. Baggert kept house for the widower and his son. There was also, in their household, an aged engineer, named Garret Jackson, who attended to the engine and boilers that operated machinery and apparatus in several small shops that surrounded the Swift homestead; for Mr. Swift did most of his work at home.

As related in the first volume of this series, entitled "Tom Swift and His Motor-Cycle," the lad had passed through some strenuous adventures. A syndicate of rich men, disappointed in a turbine motor they had acquired from a certain inventor, hired a gang of scoundrels to get possession of a turbine Mr. Swift had invented. Just before they made the attempt, however, Tom became possessed of a motor-cycle. It had belonged to a wealthy man, Mr. Wakefield Damon, of Waterford, near Lake Carlopa, which body of water adjoined the town of Shopton; but Mr. Damon had two accidents with the machine, and sold it to Tom cheap. Tom was riding his motor-cycle to Albany, to deliver his father's model of the turbine motor to a lawyer, in order to get a patent on it, when he was attacked by the gang of bad men. These included Ferguson Appleson, Anson Morse, Wilson Featherton, *alias* Simpson, Jake Burke, *alias* Happy Harry, who sometimes masqueraded as a tramp, and Tod Boreck, *alias* Murdock. These men knocked Tom unconscious, stole the valuable model and some papers, and carried the youth away in their automobile.

Later the young inventor, following a clue given him by Eradicate Sampson, an aged colored man, who, with his mule, Boomerang, went about the country doing odd jobs, got on the trail of the thieves in a deserted mansion in the woods at the upper end of the lake. Our hero, with the aid of Mr. Damon, and some friends of the latter, raided the old house, but the men escaped.

In the second book of the series, called "Tom Swift and His Motor-Boat," there was related the doings of the lad, his father and his chum, Ned Newton, on Lake Carlopa. Tom bought at auction, a motor-boat the thieves had stolen and damaged, and, fixing it up, made a speedy craft of it— so speedy, in fact that it beat the racing-boat— *Red Streak*—owned by Andy Foger. But Tom did more than race in his boat. He took his father on a tour for his health, and, during Mr. Swift's absence from home, the gang of bad men stole some of the inventor's machinery. Tom set out after them in his motor boat, but the scoundrels even managed to steal that, hoping to get possession of a peculiar and mysterious treasure in it, and Tom had considerable trouble.

Among other things he did when he had his craft, was to aid a Miss Mary Nestor, who, in her cousin's small boat, the *Dot,* was having trouble with the engine, and you shall hear more of Miss Nestor presently, for she and Tom became quite friendly. Events so shaped themselves that Andy Foger was glad to loan Tom the *Red Streak* in which to search for the stolen *Arrow,* and it was in the later craft that Tom, his father and Ned Newton had a most thrilling adventure.

They were on their way down the lake when, in the air overhead they saw a balloon on fire, with a man clinging to the trapeze. They managed to save the fellow's life, after a strenuous endeavor. The balloonist, John Sharp, was destined to play quite a part in Tom's life.

Mr. Sharp was more than an aeronaut—he was the inventor of an airship—that is, he had plans drawn for the more important parts, but he had struck a "snag of clouds," as he expressed it, and could not make the machine work. His falling in with Mr. Swift and his son seemed providential, for Tom and his father were at once interested in the project for navigating the upper air. They began a study of Mr. Sharp's plans, and the balloonist was now in a fair way to have the difficulty solved.

His airship was, primarily an aeroplane, but with a sustaining aluminum container, shaped like a cigar, and filled with a secret gas, made partly of hydrogen, being very light and powerful. It was testing the effect of this gas on a small model of the aluminum container that the explosion, told of in the first chapter, occurred. In fact it was only one of several explosions, but, as Tom said, all the while they were eliminating certain difficulties, until now the airship seemed almost a finished thing. But a few more details remained to be worked out, and Mr. Swift and his son felt that they could master these.

So it was with a feeling of no little elation, that the young inventor followed Mr. Sharp into the shop. The balloonist, it may be explained, had been invited to live with the Swifts pending the completion of the airship.

"Do you think we'll get on the right track if we put the needle valve in?" asked Tom, as he noted with satisfaction that the damage from the explosion was not great.

"I'm sure we will," answered the aeronaut. "Now let's make another model container, and try the gas again."

They set to work, with Mr. Swift helping them

occasionally, and Garret Jackson, the engineer, lending a hand whenever he was needed. All that afternoon work on the airship progressed. The joint inventors of it wanted to be sure that the sustaining gas bag, or aluminum container, would do its work properly, as this would hold them in the air, and prevent accidents, in case of a stoppage of the engine or propellers.

The aeroplane part of the airship was all but finished, and the motor, a powerful machine, of new design, built by Mr. Swift, was ready to be installed.

All that afternoon Tom, his father and Mr. Sharp labored in the shop. As it grew dusk there sounded from the house the ringing of a bell.

"Supper time," remarked Tom, laying aside a wrench. "I wish Mrs. Baggert would wait about an hour. I'd have this valve nearly done, then."

But the housekeeper was evidently not going to wait, for her voice supplemented the bell.

"Supper! Sup-per!" she called. "Come now, Mr. Swift; Tom, Mr. Sharp! I can't wait any longer! The meat and potatoes will be spoiled!"

"I s'pose we'd better go in," remarked Mr. Sharp, with something of a sigh. "We can finish to-morrow."

The shop, where certain parts of the airship

were being made, was doubly locked, and Jackson, the engineer, who was also a sort of watchman, was bidden to keep good guard, for the fear of the gang of unscrupulous men, who had escaped from jail during a great storm, was still in the minds of Mr. Swift and his son.

"And give an occasional look in the shed, where the aeroplane is," advised Mr. Sharp. "It wouldn't take much to damage that, now."

"I'll pay particular attention to it," promised the engineer. "Don't worry, Mr. Sharp."

After supper the three gathered around the table on which were spread out sheets of paper, covered with intricate figures and calculations, which Mr. Swift and the balloonist went over with care. Tom was examining some blue prints, which gave a sectional view of the proposed ship, and was making some measurements when the bell rang, and Mrs. Baggert ushered in Ned Newton, the most particular chum of the young inventor.

"Hello, Ned!" exclaimed Tom. "I was wondering what had become of you. Haven't seen you in a dog's age."

"That's right," admitted Ned. "We've been working late nights at the bank. Getting ready for the regular visit of the examiner, who usually comes along about this time. Well, how are things going; and how is the airship?" for, of course, Ned had heard of that.

"Oh, pretty good. Had another explosion to-day, I s'pose you heard."

"No, I hadn't."

"I thought everyone in town had, for Andy Foger and his two cronies were on hand, and they usually tell all they know."

"Oh, Andy Foger! He makes me sick! He was scooting up the street in his auto just as I was coming in, 'honking-honking' his horn to beat the band! You'd think no one ever had an auto but him. He certainly was going fast."

"Wait until I get in our airship," predicted Tom. "Then I'll show you what speed is!"

"Do you really think it will go fast?"

"Of course it will! Fast enough to catch Anson Morse and his crowd of scoundrels if we could get on their track."

"Why, I thought they were in jail," replied Ned, in some surprise. "Weren't they arrested after they stole your boat?"

"Yes, and put in jail, but they managed to get out, and now they're free to make trouble for us again."

"Are you sure they're out of jail?" asked Ned, and Tom noted that his chum's face wore an odd look.

"Sure? Of course I am. But why do you ask?"

Ned did not answer for a moment. He glanced at Tom's father, and the young inventor understood. Mr. Swift was getting rather along in age, and his long years of brain work had made him nervous. He had a great fear of Morse and his gang, for they had made much trouble for him in the past. Tom appreciated his chum's hesitancy, and guessed that Ned had something to say that he did not want Mr. Swift to hear.

"Come on up to my room, Ned. I've got something I want to show you," exclaimed Tom, after a pause.

The two lads left the room, Tom glancing apprehensively at his father. But Mr. Swift was so engrossed, together with the aeronaut, in making some calculations regarding wind pressure, that it is doubtful if either of the men were aware that the boys had gone.

"Now what is it, Ned?" demanded our hero, when they were safe in his apartment. "Something's up. I can tell by your manner. What is it?"

"Maybe it's nothing at all," went on his chum. "If I had known, though that those men had gotten out of jail, I would have paid more attention to what I saw to-night, as I was leaving the bank to come here."

"What did you see?" demanded Tom, and his manner, which had been calm, became somewhat excited.

"Well, you know I've been helping the paying-teller straighten up his books," went on the young bank employee, "and when I came out to-night, after working for several hours, I was glad enough to hurry away from the 'slave-den,' as I call it. I almost ran up the street, not looking where I was going, when, just as I turned the corner, I bumped into a man."

"Nothing suspicious or wonderful in that," commented Tom. "I've often run into people."

"Wait," advised Ned. "To save myself from falling I grabbed the man's arm. He did the same to me, and there we stood, for a moment, right under a gas lamp. I looked down at his hands, and I saw that on the little finger of the left one there was tattooed a blue ring, and——"

"Happy Harry—the tramp!" exclaimed Tom, now much excited. "That's where he wears a tattooed ring!"

"That's what I thought you had told me," resumed Ned, "but I didn't pay any attention to it at the time, as I had no idea that the men were out of jail."

"Well, what else happened?" inquired Tom.

"Not much more. I apologized to the man, and he to me, and we let go of each other."

"Are you sure about the ring on his finger?"

"Positive. His hand was right in the light. But wait, that isn't all. I hurried on, not thinking much about it, when, I saw another man step out of the dark shadows of Peterby's grocery, just beyond the bank. The man must have mistaken me for some one else, for he spoke to me."

"What did he say?"

"He asked me a question. It was: 'Is there any chance to-night?'"

"What did you tell him?"

"Well, I was so surprised that I didn't know what to say, and, before I could get my wits together the man had seen his mistake and hurried on. He joined the man I had collided with, and the two skipped off in the darkness. But not before a third man had come across the street, from in front of the bank, and hurried off with them."

"Well?" asked Tom, as his chum paused.

"I don't know what to think," resumed Ned "These men were certainly acting suspiciously, and, now that you tell me the Anson Morse gang is not locked up—well, it makes me feel that these men must be some of their crowd."

"Of course they are!" declared Tom positively. "That blue ring proves it!"

"I wouldn't go so far as to say that," declared Ned. "The man certainly had a blue ring tattooed on his finger—the same finger where you say Happy Harry had his. But what would the men be doing in this neighborhood? They certainly have had a lesson not to meddle with any of your things."

"No, I don't believe they are after any of dad's inventions this time. But I tell you what I do believe."

"What?"

"Those men are planning to rob the Shopton Bank, Ned! And I advise you to notify the officers. That Morse gang is one of the worst in the country," and Tom, much excited, began to pace the room, while Ned, who had not dreamed of such an outcome to his narrative, looked startled.

CHAPTER III

WHITEWASHED

"LET's tell your father, Tom," suggested Ned, after a pause. "He'll know what to do."

"No, I'd rather not," answered the young inventor quickly. "Dad has had trouble enough with these fellows, and I don't want him to worry any more. Besides, he is working on a new invention, and if I tell him about the Happy Harry gang it will take his attention from it."

"What invention is he planning now?"

"I don't know, but it's something important by the way he keeps at it. He hardly spares time to help Mr. Sharp and me on the airship. No, we'll keep this news from dad."

"Then I'll inform the bank officials, as you suggest. If the place was robbed they might blame me, if they found out I had seen the men and failed to tell them."

"Well, that gang would only be too glad to have the blame fall on some one else."

Tom little knew how near the truth he had come in his chance expression, or how soon he himself was to fall under suspicion in connection with this same band of bad men.

"I'll telephone to the president on my way home," decided Ned, "and he can notify the watchman at the bank. But do you really expect to have your airship in shape to fly soon?"

"Oh, yes. Now that we have found out our mistake about the gas, the rest will be easy."

"I think I'd like to take a trip in one myself, if it didn't go too high," ventured Ned.

"I'll remember that, when we have ours completed," promised his chum, "and I'll take you for a spin."

The boys talked for perhaps an hour longer, mostly about the airship, for it was the latest mechanical affair in which Tom was interested, and, naturally, foremost in his thoughts. Then Ned went home first, however, telephoning from Tom's house to the bank president about having seen the suspicious men. That official thanked his young employee, and said he would take all necessary precautions. The telephone message was not sent until Mr. Swift was out of hearing, as Tom was determined that his father should have no unnecessary worry about the unscrupulous men. As

it was, the news that the gang was out of jail
had caused the aged inventor some alarm.

It was not without some anxiety that Tom
arose the next morning, fearing he would hear
news that the bank had been broken into, but no
such alarming report circulated in Shopton.   In
fact having made some inquiries that day of Ned,
he learned that no trace had been seen of the
mysterious men.   The police had been on the lookout, but they had seen nothing of them.

"Maybe, after all, they weren't the same ones,"
suggested Ned, when he paid Tom another visit
the next night.

"Well, of course it's possible that they weren't,"
admitted the young inventor.   "I'd be very glad
to think so.   Even if they were, your encounter
with them may have scared them off; and that
would be a good thing."

The next two weeks were busy ones for Tom
and Mr. Sharp.   Aided occasionally by Mr. Swift,
and with Garret Jackson, the engineer, to lend
a hand whenever needed, the aeronaut and the
owner of the speedy *Arrow* made considerable
progress on their airship.

"What is your father so busy over?" asked Mr.
Sharp one day, when the new aluminum gas
holder was about completed.

"I don't know," answered Tom, with a somewhat puzzled air. "He doesn't seem to want to talk about it, even to me. He says it will revolutionize travel along a certain line, but whether he is working on an airship that will rival ours, or a new automobile, I can't make out. He'll tell us in good time. But when do you think we will finish the—well, I don't know what to call it— I mean our aeroplane?"

"Oh, in about a month now. That's so, though, we haven't a name for it. But we'll christen it after it's completed. Now if you'll tighten up some of those bolts I'll get the gas generating apparatus in readiness for another test."

A short description of the new airship may not be out of place now. It was built after plans Mr. Sharp had shown to Tom and his father soon after the thrilling rescue of the aeronaut from the blazing balloon over Lake Carlopa. The general idea of the airship was that of the familiar aeroplane, but in addition to the sustaining surfaces of the planes, there was an aluminum, cigar-shaped tank, holding a new and very powerful gas, which would serve to keep the ship afloat even when not in motion.

Two sets of planes, one above the other, were used, bringing the airship into the biplane class. There were also two large propellers, one in front and the other at the rear. These were carefully made, of different layers of wood "built up" as they are called, to make them stronger. They were eight feet in diameter, and driven by a twenty-cylinder, air-cooled, motor, whirled around at the rate of fifteen hundred revolutions a minute. When operated at full speed the airship was capable of making eighty miles an hour, against a moderate wind.

But if the use of the peculiarly-shaped planes and the gas container, with the secret but powerful vapor in it were something new in airship construction, so was the car in which the operator and travelers were to live during a voyage. It was a complete living room, with the engine and other apparatus, including that for generating the gas, in a separate compartment, and the whole was the combined work of Tom and Mr. Sharp. There were accommodations for five persons, with sleeping berths, a small galley or kitchen, where food could be prepared, and several easy chairs where the travelers could rest in comfort while skimming along high in the air, as fast as the fastest railroad train.

There was room enough to carry stores for a voyage of a week or more, and enough gas could be manufactured aboard the ship, in addition to that taken in the aluminum case before starting, to sustain the ship for two weeks. The engine, steering apparatus, and the gas machine were within easy reach and control of the pilot, who was to be stationed in a small room in the "bow" of the ship. An electric stove served to warm the interior of the car, and also provided means for cooking the food.

The airship could be launched either by starting it along the ground, on rubber-tired wheels, as is done in the case of the ordinary aeroplane, or it could be lifted by the gas, just as is done with a balloon. In short there were many novel features about the ship.

The gas test, which took place a few days later, showed that the young inventor and Mr. Sharp had made no mistake this time. No explosion followed, the needle valve controlling the powerful vapor perfectly.

"Well," remarked Mr. Sharp, one afternoon, "I think we shall put the ship together next week. Tom, and have a trial flight. We shall need a few more aluminum bolts, though, and if you don't mind you might jump on your motor-cycle and run to Mansburg for them. Merton's machine shop ought to have some."

Mansburg was the nearest large city to Shopton, and Merton was a machinist who frequently did work for Mr. Swift.

"All right," agreed Tom. "I'll start now. How many will you need?"

"Oh, a couple of dozen."

Tom started off, wheeling his cycle from the shed where it was kept. As he passed the building where the big frame of the airship, with the planes and aluminum bag had been assembled, he looked in.

"We'll soon be flying through the clouds on your back," he remarked, speaking to the apparatus as if it could understand. "I guess we'll smash some records, too, if that engine works as well when it's installed as it does now."

Tom had purchased the bolts, and was on his way back with them, when, as he passed through one of the outlying streets of Mansburg, something went wrong with his motor-cycle. He got off to adjust it, finding that it was only a trifling matter, which he soon put right, when he was aware of a man standing, observing him. Without looking up at the man's face, the young inventor was unpleasantly aware of a sharp scrutiny. He could hardly explain it, but it seemed as if the man had evil intentions toward him, and it was not altogether unexpected on Tom's part, when, looking up, he saw staring at him, Anson Morse, the leader of the gang of men who had caused such trouble for him.

"Oh, it's you; is it?" asked Morse, an ugly scowl on his face. "I thought I recognized you." He moved nearer to Tom, who straightened up, and stood leaning on his wheel.

"Yes; it's me," admitted the lad.

"I've been looking for you," went on Morse. "I'm not done with you yet, nor your father, either."

"Aren't you?" asked Tom, trying to speak coolly, though his heart was beating rather faster than usual. Morse had spoken in a threatening manner, and, as the youth looked up and down the street he saw that it was deserted; nor were there any houses near.

"No, I'm not," snapped the man. "You got me and my friends in a lot of trouble, and——"

"You didn't get half what you deserved!" burst out Tom, indignant at the thought of what he and his father had suffered at the hands of the gang. "You ought to be in jail now, instead of out; and if I could see a policeman, I'd have you arrested for threatening me! That's against the law!"

"Huh! I s'pose you think you know lots about the law," sneered Morse. "Well, I tell you one thing; if you make any further trouble for me, I'll——"

"I'll make all the trouble I can!" cried Tom,

and he boldly faced the angry man. "I'm not afraid of you!"

"You'd better be!" and Morse spoke in a vindictive manner. "We'll get even with you yet, Tom Swift. In fact I've a good notion now to give you a good thrashing for what you've done."

Before Tom was aware of the man's intention, Morse had stepped quickly into the street, where the lad stood beside his wheel, and grasped him by the shoulder. He gave Tom a vicious shake.

"Take your hand off me!" cried Tom, who was hampered by having to hold up his heavy machine.

"I will when I've given you what I owe you!" retorted the scoundrel. "I'm going to have satisfaction now if I never——"

At that instant there came from down the street the sound of a rattling and bumping. Tom looked up quickly, and saw approaching a rattletrap of a wagon, drawn by a big, loose-jointed mule, the large ears of which were flapping to and fro. The animal was advancing rapidly, in response to blows and words from the colored driver, and, before the uplifted fist of Morse could fall on Tom's head, the outfit was opposite them.

"Hold on dar, mistah! Hold on!" cried the colored man in the wagon. "What are yo' doin' to mah friend, Mistah Swift?"

"None of your business!" snapped Morse. "You drive on and let me manage this affair if you don't want trouble! Who are you anyhow?"

"Why doan't yo' know me?" asked the colored man, at whom Tom looked gratefully. "I's Eradicate Sampson, an' dish yeah am mah mule, Boomerang. Whoa, Boomerang! I reckon yo' an' I better take a hand in dish yeah argument."

"Not unless you want trouble!" cried Morse.

"I doan't mind trouble, not in de leastest," answered Eradicate cheerfully. "Me an' Boomerang has had lots of trouble. We's used to it. No, Mistah Man, you'd better let go ob mah friend, Mistah Swift, if yo' doan't want trouble yo' ownse'f."

"Drive on, and mind your business!" cried Morse, now unreasoningly angry. "This is my affair," and he gave Tom a shake.

Our hero was not going to submit tamely, however. He had one hand free, and raised to strike Morse, but the latter, letting go his hold on the lad's shoulder, grasped with that hand, the fist which the young inventor had raised. Then, with his other hand, the scoundrel was about to hit Tom.

"Break away fom him, Mistah Swift!" directed the colored man. "Yo' can fight him, den!"

"I guess he'll have his own troubles doing that," sneered Morse.

"Not ef I help him," answered Eradicate promptly, as he climbed back off the seat, into the body of his ramshackle vehicle.

"Don't you interfere with me!" stormed the man.

An instant later Tom broke away from his tormentor, and laid his motor-cycle on the ground, in order to have both hands free for the attack he felt would follow.

"Ha! You think you're going to escape, do you?" cried Morse, as he started toward Tom, his eyes blazing. "I'll show you who you're dealing with!"

"Yes, an' I reckon I'll show yo' suffin yo' ain't lookin' fer!" suddenly cried Eradicate.

With a quick motion he picked up a pail of white-wash from his wagon, and, with sure aim, emptied the contents of the bucket over Morse, who was rushing at Tom. The white fluid spread over the man from head to foot, enveloping him as in a white shroud, and his advance was instantly checked.

"Dar! I reckon dat's de quickest white-washin' job I done in some time!" chuckled Eradicate, as he grasped his long handled brush, and clambered down from the wagon, ready for a renewal of the hostilities on the part of Morse. "De bestest white-washin' job I done in some time; yais, sah!"

CHAPTER IV.

A TRIAL TRIP

THERE was no fear that Anson Morse would return to the attack. Blinded by the whitewash which ran in his eyes, but which, being slaked, did not burn him, he grouped blindly about, pawing the air with his outstretched hands.

"You wait! You wait! You'll suffer for this!" he spluttered, as soon as he could free his mouth from the trickling fluid. Then, wiping it from his face, with his hands, as best he could, he shook his fist at Tom. "I'll pay you and that black rascal back!" he cried. "You wait!"

"I hopes yo' pays me soon," answered Eradicate, "'case as how dat whitewash was wuff twenty-five cents, an' I got t' go git mo' to finish doin' a chicken coop I'm wurkin' on. Whoa, dar Boomerang. Dere ain't goin' t' be no mo' trouble I reckon."

Morse did not reply. He had been most unexpectedly repulsed, and, with the whitewash dripping from his garments, he turned and fairly ran toward a strip of woodland that bordered the highway at that place.

Tom approached the colored man, and held out a welcoming hand.

"I don't know what I'd done if you hadn't come along, Rad," the lad said. "That fellow was desperate, and this was a lonely spot to be attacked. Your whitewash came in mighty handy."

"Yais, sah, Mistah Swift, dat's what it done. I knowed I could use it on him, ef he got too obstreperous, an' dat's what he done. But I were goin' to fight him wif mah bresh, ef he'd made any more trouble."

"Oh, I fancy we have seen the last of him for some time," said Tom, but he looked worried. It was evident that the Happy Harry gang was still hanging around the neighborhood of Shopton, and the fact that Morse was bold enough to attack our hero in broad day-light argued that he felt little fear of the authorities.

"Ef yo' wants t' catch him, Mistah Swift," went on Eradicate, "yo' kin trace him by de whitewash what drops offen him," and he pointed to a trail of white drops which showed the path Morse had taken.

"No, the less I have to do with him the better

I like it," answered the lad. "But I can't thank you enough, Rad. You have helped me out of difficulties several times now. You put me on the trail of the men in the deserted mansion, you warned me of the log Andy Foger placed across the road, and now you have saved me from Morse."

"Oh, dat's nuffin, Mistah Swift. Yo' has suah done lots fo' me. 'Sides, mah mule, Boomerang, am entitled t' de most credit dish yeah time. I were comin' down de street, on mah way t' a whitewashin' job, when I seen yo', an yo' lickity-split machine," for so Eradicate designated a motor-cycle. "I knowed it were yo', an' I didn't laik de looks ob dat man. Den I see he had hold ob you, an' I t'ought he were a burglar. So I yelled t' Boomerang t' hurry up. Now, mostly, when I wants Boomerang t' hurry, he goes slow, an' when I wants him t' go slow, he runs away. But dish yeah time he knowed he were comin' t' help yo', an' he certainly did leg it, dat's what he done! He run laik he were goin' home t' a stable full ob oats, an' dat's how I got heah so quick. Den I t'ought ob de whitewash, an' I jest used it."

"It was the most effective weapon you could have used," said Tom, gratefully.

"Deed no, Mistah Swift, I didn't hab no weapon," spoke Eradicate earnestly. "I ain't eben got mah razor, 'case I left it home. I didn't hab no weapon at all. I jest used de whitewash, laik yo' seen me."

"That's what I meant," answered Tom, trying not to laugh at the simple negro's misunderstanding. "I'm ever so much obliged to you, just the same, and here's a half dollar to pay for the whitewash."

"Oh, no, Mistah Swift, I doan't want t' take it. I kin make mo' whitewash."

But Tom insisted, and picked up his machine to sprint for home. Eradicate started to tell over again, how he urged Boomerang on, but the lad had no time to listen.

"But I didn't hab no weapon, Mistah Swift, no indeedy, none at all, not even mah razor," repeated Eradicate. "Only de pail ob whitewash. That is, lessen yo' calls mah bresh a weapon."

"Well, it's a sort of one," admitted Tom, with a laugh as he started his machine. "Come around next week, Rad. We have some dirt eradicating for you to attend to."

"Deed an' I will, Mistah Swift. Eradicate is mah name, an' I eradicates de dirt. But dat man suah did look odd, wif dat pail ob whitewash all ober him. He suah did look most extraordinarily.

Gidap, Boomerang. See if yo' can break some mo' speed records now."

But the mule appeared to be satisfied with what he had done, and, as he rode off, Tom looked back to see the colored man laboring to get the sleepy animal started.

The lad did not tell his father of the adventure with Morse, but he related the occurrence to Mr. Sharp.

"I'd like to get hold of that scoundrel, and the others in the gang!" exclaimed the balloonist. "I'd take him up in the airship, and drop him down into the lake. He's a bad man. So are the others. Wonder what they want around here?"

"That's what's puzzling me," admitted Tom. "I hope dad doesn't hear about them or he will be sure to worry; and maybe it will interfere with his new ideas."

"He hasn't told you yet what he's engaged in inventing; has he?"

"No, and I don't like to ask him. He said the other day, though, that it would rival our airship, but in a different way."

"I wonder what he meant?"

"It's hard to say. But I don't believe he can invent anything that will go ahead of our craft, even if he is my own father, and the best one in the world," said Tom, half jokingly. "Well, I got the bolts, now let's get to work. I'm anxious for a trial trip."

"No more than I am. I want to see if my ideas will work out in practice as well as they do in theory."

For a week or more Tom and Mr. Sharp labored on the airship, with Mr. Jackson to help them. The motor, with its twenty cylinders, was installed, and the big aluminum holder fastened to the frame of the planes. The rudders, one to control the elevation and depression of the craft, and the other to direct its flight to the right or left, were attached, and the steering wheel, as well as the levers regulating the motor were put in place.

"About all that remains to be done now," said the aeronaut one night, as he and Tom stood in the big shed, looking at their creation, "is to fit up the car, and paint the machine."

"Can't we make a trial trip before we fit up the car ready for a long flight?" asked the young inventor.

"Yes, but I wouldn't like to go out without painting the ship. Some parts of it might rust if we get into the moist, cloudy, upper regions."

"Then let's paint it to-morrow, and, as soon as it's dry we'll have a test."

"All right. I'll mix the paint the first thing in the morning."

It took two days to paint the machine, for much care had to be used, and, when it was finished Tom looked admiringly up at it.

"We ought to name it," suggested Mr. Sharp, as he removed a bit of paint from the end of the nose.

"To be sure," agreed Tom. "And—hold on, I have the very name for it—*Red Cloud!*"

"*Red Cloud?*" questioned Mr. Sharp.

"Yes!" exclaimed Tom, with enthusiasm. "It's painted red—at least the big, aluminum gas container is—and we hope to go above the clouds in it. Why not *Red Cloud?*"

"That's what it shall be!" conceded the balloonist. "If I had a bottle of malted milk, or something like that, I'd christen it."

"We ought to have a young lady to do that part," suggested Tom. "They always have young ladies to name ships."

"Were you thinking of any particular young lady?" asked Mr. Sharp softly, and Tom blushed as he replied:

"Oh no—of course that is—well—Oh, hang it, christen it yourself, and let me alone," he finished.

"Well, in the absence of Miss Mary Nestor, who, I think, would be the best one for the cere-

mony," said Mr. Sharp, with a twinkle in his
eyes, "I christen thee *Red Cloud*," and with that
he sprinkled some water on the pointed nose of
the red aluminum gas bag, for the aeronaut and
Tom were on a high staging, on a level with the
upper part of the airship.

"*Red Cloud* it is!" cried Tom, enthusiastically.
"Now, to-morrow we'll see what it can do."

The day of the test proved all that could be
desired in the way of weather. The fact that an
airship was being constructed in the Swift shops
had been kept as secret as possible, but of course
many in Shopton knew of it, for Andy Foger had
spread the tidings.

"I hope we won't have a crowd around to see
us go up," said Tom, as he and Mr. Sharp went
to the shed to get the *Red Cloud* in readiness
for the trial. "I shouldn't want to have them
laugh at us, if we fail to rise."

"Don't worry. We'll go up all right," declared Mr. Sharp. "The only thing I'm at all
worried about is our speed. I want to go fast, but
we may not be able to until our motor gets
'tuned-up.' But we'll rise."

The gas machine had already been started, and
the vapor was hissing inside the big aluminum
holder. It was decided to try to go up under
the lifting power of the gas, and not use the aero-

plane feature for sending aloft the ship, as there was hardly room, around the shops, for a good start.

When enough of the vapor had been generated to make the airship buoyant, the big doors of the shed were opened, and Tom and Mr. Sharp, with the aid of Garret and Mr. Swift, shoved it slowly out.

"There it is! There she comes!" cried several voices outside the high fence that surrounded the Swift property. "They're going up!"

"Andy Foger is in that bunch," remarked Tom with a grim smile. "I hope we don't fail."

"We won't. Don't worry," advised Mr. Sharp.

The shouts outside the fence increased. It was evident that quite a crowd of boys, as well as men, had collected, though it was early in the morning. Somehow, news of the test had leaked out.

The ship continued to get lighter and lighter as more gas was generated. It was held down by ropes, fastened to stakes driven in the ground. Mr. Sharp entered the big car that was suspended below the aeroplanes.

"Come on, Tom," the aeronaut called. "We're almost ready to fly. Will you come too, Mr. Swift, and Garret?"

"Some other time," promised the aged inventor. "It looks as though you were going to succeed, though. I'll wait, however, until after the test before I venture."

"How about you, Garret?" asked Tom of the engineer, as the young inventor climbed into the car.

"The ground is good enough for me," was the answer, with a smile. "Broken bones don't mend so easily when you're past sixty-five."

"But we're not going to fall!' declared Mr. Sharp. "All ready, Tom. Cast off! Here we go!"

The restraining ropes were quickly cast aside. Slowly at first, and then with a rush, as though feeling more and more sure of herself, the *Red Cloud* arose in the air like a gigantic bird of scarlet plumage. Up and up it went, higher than the house, higher than the big shed where it had been built, higher, higher, higher!

"There she is!" cried the shrill voices of the boys in the meadow, and the hoarser tones of the men mingled with them.

"Hurrah!" called Tom softly to the balloonist. "We're off!" and he waved his hand to his father and Garret.

"I told you so," spoke Mr. Sharp confidently. "I'm going to start the propellers in a minute."

"Oh, dear me, goodness sakes alive!" cried

Mrs. Baggert, the housekeeper, running from the house and wringing her hands. "I'm sure they'll fall!"

She looked up apprehensively, but Tom only waved his hand to her, and threw her a kiss. Clearly he had no fears, though it was the first time he had ever been in an airship. Mr. Sharp was as calm and collected as an ocean captain making his hundredth trip across the Atlantic.

"Throw on the main switch," he called to our hero, and Tom, moving to amidships in the car, did as directed. Mr. Sharp pulled several levers, adjusted some valves, and then, with a rattle and bang, the huge, twenty-cylinder motor started.

Waiting a moment to see that it was running smoothly, Mr. Sharp grasped the steering wheel. Then, with a quick motion he threw the two propellers in gear. They began to whirl around rapidly.

"Here we go!" cried Tom, and, sure enough, the *Red Cloud*, now five hundred feet in the air, shot forward, like a boat on the water, only with such a smooth, gliding, easy motion, that it seemed like being borne along on a cloud.

"She works! She works!" cried the balloonist. "Now to try our elevation rudder," and, as the *Red Cloud* gathered speed, he tilted the small planes which sent the craft up or down, according to the manner in which they were tilted. The next instant the airship was pointed at an angle toward the clouds, and shooting along at swift speed, while, from below came the admiring cheers of the crowd of boys and men.

CHAPTER V

COLLIDING WITH A TOWER

"She seems to work," observed Tom, looking from where he was stationed near some electrical switches, toward Mr. Sharp.

"Of course she does," replied the aeronaut. "I knew it would, but I wasn't so sure that it would scoot along in this fashion. We're making pretty good speed, but we'll do better when the motor gets to running smoother."

"How high up are we?" asked Tom.

The balloonist glanced at several gauges near the steering wheel.

"A little short of three thousand feet," he answered. "Do you want to go higher?"

"No—no—I—I guess not," was Tom's answer. He halted over the works, and his breath came in gasps.

"Don't get alarmed," called Mr. Sharp quickly, noting that his companion was in distress because of the high altitude. "That always happens to persons who go into a thin air for the first time; just as if you had climbed a high mountain. Breathe as slowly as you can, and swallow frequently. That will relieve the pressure on your ear drums. I'll send the ship lower."

Tom did as he was advised, and the aeronaut, deflecting the rudder, sent the *Red Cloud* on a downward slant. Tom at once felt relieved, both because the action of swallowing equalized the pressure on the ear drums, and because the airship was soon in a more dense atmosphere, more like that of the earth.

"How are you now?" asked the man of the lad, as the craft was again on an even keel.

"All right," replied Tom, briskly. "I didn't know what ailed me at first."

"I was troubled the same way when I first went up in a balloon," commented Mr. Sharp. "We'll run along for a few miles, at an elevation of about five hundred feet, and then we'll go to within a hundred feet of the earth, and see how the *Red Cloud* behaves under different conditions. Take a look below and see what you think of it."

Tom looked low, through one of several plate-glass windows in the floor of the car. He gave a gasp of astonishment.

"Why! We're right over Lake Carlopa!" he gasped.

"Of course," admitted Mr. Sharp with a laugh. "And I'm glad to say that we're better off than when I was last in the air over this same body of water," and he could scarcely repress a shudder as he thought of his perilous position in the blazing balloon, as related in detail in "Tom Swift and His Motor-Boat."

The lake was spread out below the navigators of the air like some mirror of silver in a setting of green fields. Tom could see a winding river, that flowed into the lake, and he noted towns, villages, and even distant cities, interspersed here and there with broad farms or patches of woodlands, like a bird's-eye view of a stretch of country.

"This is great!" he exclaimed, with enthusiasm. "I wouldn't miss this for the world!"

"Oh, you haven't begun to see things yet," replied Mr. Sharp. "Wait until we take a long trip, which we'll do soon, as this ship is behaving much better than I dared to hope. Well, we're five hundred feet high now, and I'll run along at that elevation for a while."

Objects on the earth became more distinct now, and Tom could observe excited throngs running along and pointing upward. They were several miles from Shopton, and the machinery was running smoothly; the motor, with its many cylinders purring like a big cat.

"We could have lunch, if we'd brought along anything to eat," observed Tom.

"Yes," assented his companion. "But I think we'll go back now. Your father may be anxious. Just come here, Tom, and I'll show you how to steer. I'm going down a short distance. "

He depressed the rudder, and the *Red Cloud* shot earthward. Then, as the airship was turned about, the young inventor was allowed to try his hand at managing it. He said, afterward, that it was like guiding a fleecy cloud.

"Point her straight for Shopton," counseled Mr. Sharp, when he had explained the various wheels and levers to the lad.

"Straight she is," answered the lad, imitating a sailor's reply. "Oh, but this is great! It beats even my motor-boat!"

"It goes considerably faster, at all events," remarked Mr. Sharp. "Keep her steady now, while I take a look at the engine. I want to be sure it doesn't run hot."

He went aft, where all the machinery in the car was located, and Tom was left alone in the small pilot house. He felt a thrill as he looked down at the earth beneath him, and saw the crowds of wonder-gazers pointing at the great, red airship flying high over their heads. Rapidly the open fields slipped along, giving place to a large city.

"Rocksmond," murmured Tom, as he noted it. "We're about fifty miles from home, but we'll soon be back in the shed at this rate. We certainly are slipping along. A hundred and fifty feet elevation," he went on, as he looked at a gauge. I wonder if I'll ever get used to going several miles up in the air?"

He shifted the rudder a bit, to go to the left. The *Red Cloud* obeyed promptly, but, the next instant something snapped. Tom, with a startled air, looked around. He could see nothing wrong, but a moment later, the airship dipped suddenly toward the earth. Then it seemed to increase its forward speed, and, a few seconds later, was rushing straight at a tall, ornamental tower that rose from one corner of a large building.

"Mr. Sharp! Mr. Sharp!" cried the lad. "Something has happened! We're heading for that tower!"

"Steer to one side!" called the balloonist.

Tom tried, but found that the helm had become jammed. The horizontal rudder would not work, and the craft was rushing nearer and nearer, every minute, to the pile of brick and mortar.

"We're going to have a collision!" shouted Tom. "Better shut off the power!"

The two propellers were whirling around so swiftly that they looked like blurs of light. Mr. Sharp came rushing forward, and Tom relinquished the steering wheel to him. In vain did the aeronaut try to change the course of the airship. Then, with a shout to Tom to disconnect the electric switch, the man turned off the power from the motor.

But it was too late. Straight at the tower rushed the *Red Cloud*, and, a moment later had hit it a glancing blow, smashing the forward propeller, and breaking off both blades. The nose of the aluminum gas container knocked off a few bricks from the tower, and then, the ship losing way, slowly settled to the flat roof of the building.

"We're smashed!" cried Tom, with something like despair in his voice.

"That's nothing! Don't worry! It might be worse! Not the first time I've had an accident. It's only one propeller, and I can easily make another," said Mr. Sharp, in his quick, jerky sentences. He had allowed some of the gas to escape from the container, making the ship less buoyant, so that it remained on the roof.

The aeronaut and Tom looked from the windows of the car, to note if any further damage

had been done. They were just congratulating
themselves that the rudder marked the extent,
when, from a scuttle in the roof there came a
procession of young ladies, led by an elderly ma-
tron, wearing spectacles and having a very determined, bristling air.

"Well, I must say, this is a very unceremoni-
ous proceeding!" exclaimed the spectacled woman.
"Pray, gentlemen, to what are we indebted for
this honor?"

"It was an accident, ma'am," replied Mr.
Sharp, removing his hat, and bowing. A mere
accident!"

"Humph! I suppose it was an accident that
the tower of this building was damaged, if not
absolutely loosened at the foundations. You will
have to pay the damages!" Then turning, and
seeing about two score of young ladies behind her
on the flat roof, each young lady eying with astonishment, not unmixed with admiration, the
airship, the elderly one added: "Pupils! To your
rooms at once! How dare you leave without permission?"

"Oh, Miss Perkman!" exclaimed a voice, at the
sound of which Tom started. "Mayn't we see
the airship? It will be useful in our natural
philosophy study!"

Tom looked at the young lady who had spoken.

"Mary Nestor!" he exclaimed.

"Tom—I mean Mr. Swift!" she rejoined. "How in the world did you get here?"

"I was going to ask you the same question," retorted the lad. "We flew here."

"Young ladies! Silence!" cried Miss Perkman, who was evidently the principal of the school. "The idea of any one of you daring to speak to these—these persons—without my permission, and without an introduction! I shall make them pay heavily for damaging my seminary," she added, as she strode toward Mr. Sharp, who, by this time, was out of the car. "To your rooms at once!" Miss Perkman ordered again, but not a young lady moved. The airship was too much of an attraction for them.

CHAPTER VI

GETTING OFF THE ROOF

For a few minutes Mr. Sharp was so engrossed with looking underneath the craft, to ascertain in what condition the various planes and braces were, that he paid little attention to the old maid school principal, after his first greeting. But Miss Perkman was not a person to be ignored.

"I want pay for the damage to the tower of my school," she went on. "I could also demand damages for trespassing on my roof, but I will refrain in this case. Young ladies, *will* you go to your rooms?" she demanded.

"Oh, please, let us stay," pleaded Mary Nestor, beside whom Tom now stood. "Perhaps Professor Swift will lecture on clouds and air currents and—and such things as that," the girl went on slyly, smiling at the somewhat embarrassed lad.

"Ahem! If there is a professor present, perhaps it *might* be a good idea to absorb some knowledge," admitted the old maid, and, unconsciously, she smoothed her hair, and settled her gold spectacles straighter on her nose. "Professor, I will delay collecting damages on behalf of the Rocksmond Young Ladies Seminary, while you deliver a lecture on air currents," she went on, addressing herself to Mr. Sharp.

"Oh, I'm not a professor," he said quickly. "I'm a professional balloonist, parachute jumper. Give exhibitions at county fairs. Leap for life, and all that sort of thing. I guess you mean my friend. He's smart enough for a professor. Invented a lot of things. How much is the damage?"

"No professor?" cried Miss Perkman indignantly. "Why I understood from Miss Nestor that she called some one professor."

"I was referring to my friend, Mr. Swift," said Mary. "His father's a professor, anyhow, isn't he, Tom? I mean Mr. Swift!"

"I believe he has a degree, but he never uses it," was the lad's answer.

"Ha! Then I have been deceived! There is no professor present!" and the old maid drew herself up as though desirous of punishing some one. "Young ladies, for the last time, I order you to your rooms," and, with a dramatic gesture she pointed to the scuttle through which the procession had come.

"Say something, Tom—I mean Mr. Swift," appealed Mary Nestor, in a whisper, to our hero. "Can't you give some sort of a lecture? The girls are just crazy to hear about the airship, and this ogress won't let us. Say something!"

"I—I don't know what to say," stammered Tom.

But he was saved the necessity for just then several women, evidently other teachers, came out on the roof.

"Oh, an airship!" exclaimed one. "How lovely! We thought it was an earthquake, and we were afraid to come up for quite a while. But an airship! I've always wanted to see one, and now I have an opportunity. It will be just the thing for my physical geography and natural history class. Young ladies, attention, and I will explain certain things to you."

"Miss Delafield, do you understand enough about an airship to lecture on one?" asked Miss Perkman smartly.

"Enough so that my class may benefit," answered the other teacher, who was quite pretty.

"Ahem! That is sufficient, and a different matter," conceded Miss Perkman. "Young ladies, give your undivided attention to Miss Dela-

field, and I trust you will profit by what she tells
you. Meanwhile I wish to have some conversa-
tion concerning damages with the persons who so
unceremoniously visited us. It is a shame that
the pupils of the Rocksmond Seminary should be
disturbed at their studies. Sir, I wish to talk with
you," and the principal pointed a long, straight
finger at Mr. Sharp.

"Young ladies, attention!" called Miss Delafield. "You will observe the large red body at
the top, that is—"

"I'd rather have *you* explain it," whispered
Mary Nestor to Tom. "Come on, slip around to
the other side. May I bring a few of my friends
with me? I can't bear Miss Delafield. She
thinks she knows everything. She won't see us
if we slip around."

"I shall be delighted," replied Tom, "only I
fear I may have to help Mr. Sharp out of this
trouble."

"Don't worry about me, Tom," said the balloonist, who overheard him. "Let me do the explaining: I'm an old hand at it. Been in trouble
before. Many a time I've had to pay damages
for coming down in a farmer's corn field. I'll
attend to the lady principal, and you can explain
things to the young ones," and, with a wink, the
jolly aeronaut stepped over to where Miss Perk-

man, in spite of her prejudice against the airship, was observing it curiously.

Glad to have the chance to talk to his young lady friend, Tom slipped to the opposite side of the car with her and a few of her intimate friends, to whom she slyly beckoned. There Tom told how the *Red Cloud* came to be built, and of his first trip in the air, while, on the opposite side, Miss Delafield lectured to the entire school on aeronautics, as she thought she knew them.

Mr. Sharp evidently did know how to "explain" matters to the irate principal, for, in a short while, she was smiling. By this time Tom had about finished his little lecture, and Miss Delafield was at the end of hers. The entire school of girls was grouped about the *Red Cloud*, curiously examining it, but Mary Nestor and her friends probably learned more than any of the others. Tom was informed that his friend had been attending the school in Rocksmond since the fall term opened.

"I little thought, when I found we were going to smash into that tower, that you were below there, studying," said the lad to the girl.

"I'm afraid I wasn't doing much studying," she confessed. "I had just a glimpse of the airship through the window, and I was wondering who was in it, when the crash came. Miss Perkman, who is nothing if not brave, at once started for the roof, and we girls all followed her. However, are you going to get the ship down?"

"I'm afraid it is going to be quite a job," admitted Tom ruefully. "Something went wrong with the machinery, or this never would have happened. As soon as Mr. Sharp has settled with your principal we'll see what we can do."

"I guess he's settled now," observed Miss Nestor. "Here he comes."

The aeronaut and Miss Perkman were approaching together, and the old maid did not seem half so angry as she had been.

"You see," Mr. Sharp was saying, "it will be a good advertisement for your school. Think of having the distinction of having harbored the powerful airship, *Red Cloud,* on your roof."

"I never thought of it in that light," admitted the principal. "Perhaps you are right. I shall put it in my next catalog."

"And, as for damages to the tower, we will pay you fifty dollars," continued the balloonist. "Do you agree to that, Mr. Swift?" he asked Tom. "I think your father, the professor, would call that fair."

"Oh, as long as this airship is partly the property of a professor, perhaps I should only take thirty-five dollars," put in Miss Perkman. "I am a great admirer of professors—I mean in a strictly educational sense," she went on, as she detected a tendency on the part of some of the young ladies to giggle.

"No, fifty dollars will be about right," went on Mr. Sharp, pulling out a well-filled wallet. "I will pay you now."

"And if you will wait I will give you a receipt," continued the principal, evidently as much appeased at the mention of a professor's title, as she was by the money.

"We're getting off cheap," the balloonist whispered to Tom, as the head of the seminary started down the scuttle to the class-rooms below.

"Maybe it's easier getting out of that difficulty than it will be to get off the roof," replied the lad.

"Don't worry. Leave that to me," the aeronaut said. It took considerable to ruffle Mr. Sharp.

With a receipt in full for the damage to the tower, and expressing the hope that, some day, in the near future, Professor Swift would do the seminary the honor of lecturing to the young lady pupils, Miss Perkman bade Mr. Sharp and Tom good-by.

"Young ladies, to your rooms!" she commanded. "You have learned enough of airships, and there may be some danger getting this one off the roof."

"Wouldn't you like to stay and take a ride in it?" Tom asked Miss Nestor.

"Indeed I would," she answered daringly. "It's better than a motor-boat. May I?"

"Some day, when we get more expert in managing it," he replied, as he shook hands with her.

"Now for some hard work," went on the young inventor to Mr. Sharp, when the roof was cleared of the last of the teachers and pupils. But the windows that gave a view of the airship in its odd position on the roof were soon filled with eager faces, while in the streets below was a great crowd, offering all manner of suggestions.

"Oh, it's not going to be such a task," said Mr. Sharp. "First we will repair the rudder and the machinery, and then we'll generate some more gas, rise and fly home."

"But the broken propeller?" objected Tom.

"We can fly with one, as well as we can with two, but not so swiftly. Don't worry. We'll come out all right," and the balloonist assumed a confident air.

It was not so difficult a problem as Tom had imagined to put the machinery in order, a simple break having impaired the working of the rudder. Then the smashed propeller was unshipped and the gas machine started. With all the pupils watching from windows, and a crowd observing from the streets and surrounding country, for word of the happening had spread, Tom and his friend prepared to ascend.

They arose as well as they had done at the shed at home, and in a little while, were floating over the school. Tom fancied he could observe a certain hand waving to him, as he peered from the window of the car—a hand in one of the school casements, but where there were so many pretty girls doing the same thing, I hardly see how Tom could pick out any certain one, though he had extraordinarily good eyesight. However, the airship was now afloat and, starting the motor, Mr. Sharp found that even with one propeller the *Red Cloud* did fairly well, making good speed.

"Now for home, to repair everything, and we'll be ready for a longer trip," the aeronaut said to the young inventor, as they turned around, and headed off before the wind, while hundreds below them cheered.

"We ought to carry spare propellers if we're going to smash into school towers," remarked Tom. "I seem to be a sort of hoodoo."

"Nonsense! It wasn't your fault at all," commented Mr. Sharp warmly. "It would have happened to me had I been steering. But we will take an extra propeller along after this."

An hour later they arrived in front of the big shed and the *Red Cloud* was safely housed. Mr. Swift was just beginning to get anxious about his son and his friend, and was glad to welcome them back.

"Now for a big trip, in about a week!" exclaimed Mr. Sharp enthusiastically. "You'll come with us, won't you, Mr. Swift?"

The inventor slowly shook his head.

"Not on a trip," he said. "I may go for a trial spin with you, but I've got too important a matter under way to venture on a long trip," and he turned away without explaining what it was. But Tom and Mr. Sharp were soon to learn.

CHAPTER VII

ANDY TRIES A TRICK

WITHOUT loss of time the young inventor and the aeronaut began to repair the damage done to the *Red Cloud* by colliding with the tower. The most important part to reconstruct was the propeller, and Mr. Sharp decided to make two, instead of one, in order to have an extra one in case of future accidents.

Tom's task was to arrange the mechanism so that, hereafter, the rudder could not become jammed, and so prevent the airship from steering properly. This the lad accomplished by a simple but effective device which, when the balloonist saw it, caused him to compliment Tom.

"That's worth patenting," he declared. "I advise you to take out papers on that."

"It seems such a simple thing," answered the youth. "And I don't see much use of spending the money for a patent. Airships aren't likely to

be so numerous that I could make anything off
that patent."

"You take my advice," insisted Mr. Sharp.
"Airships are going to be used more in the future than you have any idea of. You get that
device patented."

Tom did so, and, not many years afterward
he was glad that he had, as it brought him quite
an income.

It required several days' work on the *Red
Cloud* before it was in shape for another trial.
During the hours when he was engaged in the
big shed, helping Mr. Sharp, the young inventor
spent many minutes calling to mind the memory
of a certain fair face, and I think I need not mention any names to indicate whose face it was.

"She promised to go for a ride with me," mused
the lad. "I hope she doesn't back out. But I'll
want to learn more about managing the ship before I venture with her in it. It won't do to have
any accidents then. There's Ned Newton, too.
I must take him for a skim in the clouds. Guess
I'll invite him over some afternoon, and give him
a private view of the machine, when we get it in
shape again."

About a week after the accident at the school
Mr. Sharp remarked to Tom one afternoon:

"If the weather is good to-morrow, we'll try

another flight. Do you suppose your father will come along?"

"I don't know," answered the lad. "He seems much engrossed in something. It's unusual, too, for he most generally tells me what he is engaged upon. However, I guess he will say something about it when he gets ready."

"Well, if he doesn't feel just like coming, don't argue him. He might be nervous, and, while the ship is new, I don't want any nervous passengers aboard. I can't give them my attention and look after the running of the machinery."

"I was going to propose bringing a friend of mine over to see us make the trip to-morrow," went on the young inventor. "Ned Newton— you know him. He'd like a ride."

"Oh, I guess Ned's all right. Let him come along. We won't go very high to-morrow. After a trial rise by means of the gas, I'm going to lower the ship to the ground, and try for an elevation by means of the planes. Oh, yes, bring your friend along."

Ned Newton was delighted the next day to receive Tom's invitation, and, though a little dubious about trusting himself in an airship for the first time, finally consented to go with his chum. He got a half holiday from the bank, and, shortly after dinner went to Tom's house.

"Come on out in the shed and take a look at the *Red Cloud*," proposed the young inventor. "Mr. Sharp isn't quite ready to start yet, and I'll explain some things to you."

The big shed was deserted when the lads entered, and went to the loft where they were on a level with the big, red aluminum tank. Tom began with a description of the machinery, and Ned followed him with interest.

"Now we'll go down into the car or cabin," continued the young navigator of the air, "and I'll show you what we do when we're touring amid the clouds."

As they started to descend the flight of steps from the loft platform, a noise on the ground below attracted their attention.

"Guess that's Mr. Sharp coming," said Ned.

Tom leaned over and looked down. An instant later he grasped the arm of his chum, and motioned to him to keep silent.

"Take a look," whispered the young inventor.

"Andy Foger!" exclaimed Ned, peering over the railing.

"Yes, and Sam Snedecker and Pete Bailey are with him. They sneaked in when I left the door open. Wonder what they want?"

"Up to some mischief, I'll wager," commented Ned. "Hark! They're talking."

The two lads on the loft listened intently. Though the cronies on the ground below them did not speak loudly, their voices came plainly to the listeners.

"Let's poke a hole in their gas bag," proposed Sam. "That will make them think they're not so smart as they pretend."

"Naw, we can't do that," answered Andy.

"Why not?" declared Pete.

"Because the bag's away up in the top part of the shed, and I'm not going to climb up there."

"You're afraid," sneered Sam.

"I am not! I'll punch your face if you say that again! Besides the thing that holds the gas is made of aluminum, and we can't make a hole in it unless we take an axe, and that makes too much noise."

"We ought to play some sort of a trick on Tom Swift," proposed Pete. "He's too fresh!"

Tom shook his fist at the lads on the ground, but of course they did not see him.

"I have it!" came from Andy.

"What?" demanded his two cronies.

"We'll cut some of the guy wires from the planes and rudders. That will make the airship collapse. They'll think the wires broke from the strain. Take out your knives and saw away at the wires. Hurry, too, or they may catch us."

"You're caught now," whispered Ned to Tom. "Come on down, and give 'em a trouncing."

Tom hesitated. He looked quickly about the loft, and then a smile replaced the frown of righteous anger on his face.

"I have a better way," he said.

"What is it?"

"See that pile of dirt?" and he pointed to some refuse that had been swept up from the floor of the loft. Ned nodded. "It consists of a lot of shavings, sawdust and, what's more, a lot of soot and lampblack that we used in mixing some paint. We'll sweep the whole pile down on their heads, and make them wish they'd stayed away from this place."

"Good!" exclaimed Ned, chuckling. "Give me a broom. There's another one for you."

The two lads in the loft peered down. The red-headed, squint-eyed bully and his chums had their knives out, and were about to cut some of the important guy wires, when, at a signal from Tom, Ned, with a sweep of his broom, sent a big pile of the dirt, sawdust and lampblack down upon the heads of the conspirators. The young inventor did the same thing, and for an instant the lower part of the shed looked as if a dirt-storm had taken place there. The pile of refuse went straight down on the heads of the trio, and,

as they were looking up, in order to see to cut the
wires, they received considerable of it in their
faces.

In an instant the white countenances of the
lads were changed to black—as black as the
burnt-cork performers in a minstrel show. Then
came a series of howls.

"Wow! Who did that!"

"I'm blinded! The shed is falling down!"

"Run fellows, run!" screamed Andy. "There's
been an explosion. We'll be killed!"

At that moment the big doors of the shed were
thrown open, and Mr. Sharp came in. He started
back in astonishment at the sight of the three
grotesque figures, their faces black with the soot,
and their clothes covered with sawdust and shavings, rushing wildly around.

"That will teach you to come meddling around
here, Andy Foger!" cried Tom.

"I—I—you—you—Oh, wait—I—you—" spluttered the bully, almost speechless with rage. Sam
and Pete were wildly trying to wipe the stuff from
their faces, but only made matters worse. They
were so startled that they did not know enough
to run out of the opened doors.

"Wish we had some more stuff to put on 'em,"
remarked Ned, who was holding his sides that
ached from laughter.

"I have it!" cried Tom, and he caught up a bucket of red paint, that had been used to give the airship its brilliant hue. Running to the end of the loft Tom stood for an instant over the trio of lads who were threatening and imploring by turns.

"Here's another souvenir of your visit," shouted the young inventor, as he dashed the bucket of red paint down on the conspirators. This completed the work of the dirt and soot, and a few seconds later, each face looking like a stage Indian's ready for the war-path, the trio dashed out. They shed shavings, sawdust and lampblack at every step, and from their clothes and hands and faces dripped the carmine paint.

"Better have your pictures taken!" cried Ned, peering from an upper window.

"Yes, and send us one," added Tom, joining his chum. Andy looked up at them. He dug a mass of red paint from his left ear, removed a mass of soot from his right cheek, and, shaking his fist, which was alternately striped red and black, cried out in a rage:

"I'll get even with you yet, Tom Swift!"

"You only got what was coming to you," retorted the young inventor. "The next time you come sneaking around this airship, trying to damage it, you'll get worse, and I'll have you arrested. You've had your lesson, and don't forget it."

The red-haired bully, doubly red-haired now, had nothing more to say. There was nothing he could say, and, accompanied by his companions, he made a bee-line for the rear gate in the fence, and darted across the meadow. They were all sorry enough looking specimens, but solely through their own fault.

CHAPTER VIII

WINNING A PRIZE

"WELL, Tom, what happened?" asked Mr. Sharp, as he saw the trio running away. "Looks as if you had had an exciting time here."

"No, those fellows had all the excitement," declared Ned. "We had the fun." And the two lads proceeded to relate what had taken place.

"Tried to damage the airship, eh?" asked Mr. Sharp. "I wish I'd caught them at it, the scoundrels! But perhaps you handled them as well as I could have done."

"I guess so," assented Tom. "I must see if they did cut any of the wires."

But the young inventor and his chum had acted too quickly, and it was found that nothing had been done to the *Red Cloud*.

A little later the airship was taken out of the shed, and made ready for a trip. The gas ascension was first used, and Ned and Mr. Swift were passengers with Tom and Mr. Sharp. The ma-

chine went about a thousand feet up in the air,
and then was sent in various directions, to the
no small delight of a large crowd that gathered
in the meadow back of the swift property; for it
only required the sight of the airship looming its
bulk above the fence and buildings, to attract a
throng. It is safe to say this time, however, that
Andy Foger and his cronies were not in the
audience. They were probably too busy removing
the soot and red paint.

Although it was the first time Mr. Swift had
ever been in an airship, he evinced no great astonishment. In fact he seemed to be thinking
deeply, and on some subject not connected with
aeronautics. Tom noticed the abstraction of his
father, and shook his head. Clearly the aged inventor was not his usual self.

As for Ned Newton his delight knew no
bounds, At first he was a bit apprehensive as the
big ship went higher and higher, and swung about,
but he soon lost his fear, and enjoyed the experience as much as did Tom. The young inventor
was busy helping Mr. Sharp manage the machinery, rudders-planes and motor.

A flight of several miles was made, and Tom
was wishing they might pay another visit to the
Rocksmond Seminary, but Mr. Sharp, after com-

pleting several evolutions, designed to test the steering qualities of the craft, put back home.

"We'll land in the meadow and try rising by the planes alone," he said. In this evolution it was deemed best for Mr. Swift and Ned to alight, as there was no telling just how the craft would behave. Tom's father was very willing to get out, but Ned would have remained in, only for the desire of his friend.

With the two propellers whirring at a tremendous speed, and all the gas out of the aluminum container, the *Red Cloud* shot forward, running over the level ground of the meadow, where a starting course had been laid out.

"Clear the track!" cried Mr. Sharp, as he saw the crowd closing up in front of him. The men, boys, several girls and women made a living lane. Through this shot the craft, and then, when sufficient momentum had been obtained, Tom, at a command from the aeronaut, pulled the lever of the elevation rudder. Up into the air shot the nose of the *Red Cloud* as the wind struck the slanting surface of the planes, and, a moment later it was sailing high above the heads of the throng.

"That's the stuff!" cried Mr. Sharp. "It works as well that way as it does with the gas!"

Higher and higher it went, and then, coming

to a level keel, the craft was sent here and there, darting about like a bird, and going about in huge circles.

"Start the gas machine, and we'll come to rest in the air," said the balloonist, and Tom did so. As the powerful vapor filled the container the ship acquired a bouyancy, and there was no need of going at high speed in order to sustain it. The propellers were stopped, and the *Red Cloud* floated two thousand feet in the air, only a little distance below some fleecy, white masses from which she took her name. The demonstration was a great success. The gas was again allowed to escape, the propellers set in motion, and purely as an aeroplane, the ship was again sent forward. By means of the planes and rudders a perfect landing was made in the meadow, a short distance from where the start had been made. The crowd cheered the plucky youth and Mr. Sharp.

"Now I'm ready to go on a long trip any time you are, Tom," said the aeronaut that night.

"We'll fit up the car and get ready," agreed the youth. "How about you, dad?"

"Me? Oh, well—er—that is, you see; well, I'll think about it," and Mr. Swift went to his own room, carrying with him a package of papers, containing intricate calculations.

Tom shook his head, but said nothing. He could not understand his father's conduct.

Work was started the next day on fitting up the car, or cabin, of the airship, so that several persons could live, eat and sleep in it for two weeks, if necessary. The third day after this task had been commenced the mail brought an unusual communication to Tom and Mr. Sharp. It was from an aero club of Blakeville, a city distant about a hundred miles, and stated that a competition for aeroplanes and dirigible balloons was to be held in the course of two weeks. The affair was designed to further interest in the sport, and also to demonstrate what progress had been made in the art of conquering the air. Prizes were to be given, and the inventors of the *Red Cloud*, the achievements of which the committee of arrangements had heard, were invited to compete.

"Shall we go in for it, Tom?" asked the balloonist.

"I'm willing if you are."

"Then let's do it. We'll see how our craft shows up alongside of others. I know something of this club. It is all right, but the carnival is likely to be a small one. Once I gave a balloon exhibition for them. The managers are all right. Well, we'll have a try at it. Won't do us any harm to win a prize. Then for a long trip!"

As it was not necessary to have the car, or cabin, completely fitted up in order to compete for the prize, work in that direction was suspended for the time being, and more attention was paid to the engine, the planes and rudders. Some changes were made and, a week later the *Red Cloud* departed for Blakeville. As the rules of the contest required three passengers, Ned Newton was taken along, Mr. Swift having arranged with the bank president so that the lad could have a few days off.

The *Red Cloud* arrived at the carnival grounds in the evening, having been delayed on the trip by a broken cog wheel, which was mended in mid-air. As the three navigators approached, they saw a small machine flying around the grounds.

"Look!" cried Ned excitedly. "What a small airship."

"That's a monoplane," declared Tom, who was getting to be quite an expert.

"Yes, the same kind that was used to cross the English Channel," interjected Mr. Sharp. "They're too uncertain for my purposes, though they are all right under certain conditions."

Hardly had he spoken than a puff of wind caused the daring manipulator of the monoplane to swerve to one side. He had to make a quick descent—so rapid was it, in fact, that the tips of one of his planes was smashed.

"It'll take him a day to repair that," commented the aeronaut dryly.

The *Red Cloud* created a sensation as she slowly settled down in front of the big tent assigned to her. Tom's craft was easily the best one at the carnival, so far, though the managers said other machines were on the way.

The exhibition opened the next day, but no flights were to be attempted until the day following. Two more crafts arrived, a large triplane, and a dirigible balloon. There were many visitors to the ground, and Tom, Ned and Mr. Sharp were kept busy answering questions put by those who crowded into their tent. Toward the close of the day a fussy little Frenchman entered, and, making his way to where Tom stood, asked:

"Air you ze ownair of zis machine?"

"One of them," replied the lad.

"Ha! Sacre! Zen I challenge you to a race. I have a monoplane zat is ze swiftest evaire! One thousand francs will I wager you, zat I can fly higher and farther zan you."

"Shall we take him up, Mr. Sharp?" asked Tom.

"We'll race with him, after we get through with the club entries," decided the aeronaut. "but

not for money. It's against my principles, and
I don't believe your father would like it. Racing for prizes is a different thing."

"Well, we will devote ze money to charity,"
conceded the Frenchman. This was a different
matter, and one to which Mr. Sharp did not object, so it was arranged that a trial should take
place after the regular affairs.

That night was spent in getting the *Red Cloud*
in shape for the contests of the next day. She was
"groomed" until every wire was taut and every
cog, lever and valve working perfectly. Ned
Newton helped all he could. So much has appeared in the newspapers of the races at Blakeville that I will not devote much space here to
them. Suffice it to say that the *Red Cloud* easily
distanced the big dirigible from which much was
expected. It was a closer contest with the large
triplane, but Tom's airship won, and was given
the prize, a fine silver cup.

As the carnival was a small one, no other
craft in a class with the *Red Cloud* had been entered, so Tom and Mr. Sharp had to be con-
tent with the one race they won. There were
other contests among monoplanes and biplanes,
and the little Frenchman won two races.

"Now for ze affaire wis ze monstaire balloon
of ze rouge color!" he cried, as he alighted from

his monoplane while an assistant filled the gasolene tank. "I will in circles go around you, up and down, zis side zen ze ozzer, and presto! I am back at ze starting place, before you have begun. Zen charity shall be ze richair!"

"All right, wait and see," said Tom, easily. But, though he showed much confidence he asked Mr. Sharp in private, just before the impromptu contest: "Do you think we can beat him?"

"Well," said the aeronaut, shrugging his shoulders, "you can't tell much about the air. His machine certainly goes very fast, but too much wind will be the undoing of him, while it will only help us. And I think," he added, "that we're going to get a breeze."

It was arranged that the *Red Cloud* would start from the ground, without the use of the gas, so as to make the machines more even. At the signal off they started, the motors making a great racket. The monoplane with the little Frenchman in the seat got up first.

"Ah, ha!" he cried gaily, "I leave you in ze rear! Catch me if you can!"

"Don't let him beat us," implored Ned.

"Can't you speed her up any more?" inquired Tom of Mr. Sharp.

The aeronaut nodded grimly, and turned more gasolene into the twenty-cylindered engine. Like a flash the *Red Cloud* darted forward. But the Frenchman also increased his speed and did, actually, at first, circle around the bigger machine, for his affair was much lighter. But when he tried to repeat that feat he found that he was being left behind.

"That's the stuff! We're winning!" yelled Tom, Ned joining in the shout.

Then came a puff of wind. The monoplane had to descend, for it was in danger of turning turtle. Still the navigator was not going to give up. He flew along at a lower level. Then Mr. Sharp opened up the *Red Cloud's* engine at full speed, and it was the big machine which now sailed around the other.

"I protest! I protest!" cried the Frenchman, above the explosions of his motor. "Ze wind is too strong for me!"

Mr. Sharp said nothing, but, with a queer smile on his face he sent the airship down toward the earth. A moment later he was directly under the monoplane. Then, quickly rising, he fairly caught the Frenchman's machine on top of a square platform of the gas container, the bicycle wheels of the monoplane resting on the flat surface. And, so swiftly did the *Red Cloud* fly along that it carried the monoplane with it, to the chagrin of the French navigator.

"A trick! A trick!" he cried. "Eet is not fair!"

Then, dropping down, Mr. Sharp allowed the monoplane to proceed under its own power, while he raced on to the finish mark, winning, of course, by a large margin.

"Ha! A trick! I race you to-morrow and again to-morrow!" cried the beaten Frenchman as he alighted.

"No, thanks," answered Tom. "We've had enough. I guess charity will be satisfied."

The little Frenchman was a good loser, and paid over the money, which was given to the Blake-ville Hospital, the institution receiving it gladly.

At the request of the carnival committee, Mr. Sharp and Tom gave an exhibition of high and long flights the next day, and created no little astonishment by their daring feats.

"Well, I think we have reason to be proud of our ship," remarked Mr. Sharp that night. "We won the first contest we were ever in, and beat that speedy monoplane, which was no small thing to do, as they are very fast."

"But wait until we go on our trip," added Tom, as he looked at the cup they had won. He little realized what danger they were to meet with in the flight that was before them.

CHAPTER IX

THE RUNAWAY AUTO

HAD the inventors of the *Red Cloud* desired, they could have made considerable money by giving further exhibitions at the Blakeville Aero Carnival, and at others which were to be held in the near future at adjoining cities. The fame of the new machine had spread, and there were many invitations to compete for prizes.

But Tom and Mr. Sharp wished to try their skill in a long flight, and at the close of the Blakeville exhibition they started for Shopton, arriving there without mishap, though Tom more than half hoped that they might happen to strike the tower of a certain school. I needn't specify where.

The first thing to be done was to complete the fitting-up of the car, or cabin. No berths had, as yet, been put in, and these were first installed after the *Red Cloud* was in her shed. Then an electrical heating and cooking apparatus was fitted in; some additional machinery, tanks for carrying water, and chemicals for making the gas, boxes of provisions, various measuring instruments and other supplies were put in the proper places, until the cabin was filled almost to its capacity. Of course particular attention had been paid to the ship proper, and every portion was gone over until Mr. Sharp was sure it was in shape for a long flight.

"Now the question is," he said to Tom one evening, "who shall we take with us? You and I will go, of course, but I'd like one more. I wonder if your father can't be induced to accompany us? He seemed to like the trial trip."

"I'll ask him to-morrow," said the lad. "He's very busy to-night. If he doesn't care about it, maybe Garret Jackson will go."

"I'm afraid not. He's too timid."

"I'd like to take Ned Newton, but he can't get any more time away from the bank. I guess we'll have to depend on dad."

But, to the surprise of Tom and Mr. Sharp, the aged inventor shook his head when the subject was broached to him next day.

"Why won't you go, dad?" asked his son.

"I'll tell you," replied Mr. Swift. "I was keeping it a secret until I had made some advance in what I am engaged upon. But I don't want to go because I am on the verge of perfecting a new apparatus for submarine boats. It will revolutionize travel under the water, and I don't want to leave home until I finish it. There is another point to be considered. The government has offered a prize for an under-water boat of a new type, and I wish to try for it."

"So that's what you've been working on, eh, dad?" asked his son.

"That's it, and, much as I should like to accompany you, I don't feel free to go. My mind would be distracted, and I need to concentrate myself on this invention. It will produce the most wonderful results, I'm sure. Besides, the government prize is no small one. It is fifty thousand dollars for a successful boat."

Mr. Swift told something more about his submarine, but, as I expect to treat of that in another book, I will not dwell on it here, as I know you are anxious to learn what happened on the trip of the *Red Cloud*.

"Well," remarked Mr. Sharp, somewhat dubiously, "I wonder who we can get to go? We need someone besides you and I, Tom."

"I s'pose I could get Eradicate Sampson, and his mule Boomerange," replied the lad with a smile. "Yet I don't know—"

At that instant there was a tremendous racket

outside. The loud puffing of an automobile could be heard, but mingled with it was the crash of wood, and then the whole house seemed jarred and shaken.

"Is it an earthquake?" exclaimed Mr. Swift, springing to his feet, and rushing to the library windows.

"Something's happened!" cried Tom.

"Maybe an explosion of the airship gas!" yelled Mr. Sharp, making ready to run to the balloon shed. But there was no need. The crashing of wood ceased, and, above the puffing of an auto could be heard a voice exclaiming:

"Bless my very existence! Bless my cats and dogs! Good gracious! But I never meant to do this!"

Tom, his father and Mr. Sharp rushed to the long, low windows that opened on the veranda. There, on the porch, which it had mounted by way of the steps, tearing away part of the railing, was a large touring car; and, sitting at the steering wheel, in a dazed sort of manner, was Mr. Wakefield Damon.

"Bless my shirt studs!" he went on feebly. "But I have done it now!"

"What's the matter?" cried Tom, hastening up to him. "What happened? Are you hurt?"

"Hurt? Not a bit of it! Bless my moonstone!

It's the most lucky escape I ever had! But I've
damaged your porch, and I haven't done my machine any good. Do you see anything of another
machine chasing me?"

Tom looked puzzled, but glanced up and down
the road. Far down the highway could be dis-
cerned a cloud of dust, and, from the midst of
it came a faint "chug-chug."

"Looks like an auto down there," he said.

"Thank goodness! Bless my trousers, but I've
escaped 'em!" cried the eccentric man from whom
Tom had purchased his motor-cycle.

"Escaped who?" asked Mr. Swift.

"Those men. They were after me. But I may
as well get out and explain. Dear me! However will I ever get my car off your porch?" and
Mr. Damon seemed quite distressed.

"Never mind," answered Tom. "We can manage that. Tell us what happened."

"Exactly," replied Mr. Damon, growing calm-
er, "Bless my shoe buttons, but I had a fright—
two of them, in fact.

"You see," he went on, "I was out partly on
pleasure and partly on business. The pleasure
consisted in riding in my auto, which my physician recommended for my health. The business consisted in bringing to the Shopton Bank a
large amount of cash. Well, I deposited it all

right, but, as I came out I saw some men hanging around. I didn't like their looks, and I saw
them eyeing me rather sharply. I thought I had
seen them before and, sure enough I had. Two
of the men belonged to that Happy Harry gang.
I——"

Tom made a quick motion of a caution, pointing
to his father, but it was not necessary, as Mr.
Swift was absently-mindedly calculating on a
piece of paper he had taken from his pocket, and
had not heard what Mr. Damon said. The latter,
however, knew what Tom meant, and went on.

"Well, I didn't like the looks of these men,
and when I saw them sizing me up, evidently
thinking I had drawn money out instead of putting it in, I decided to give them the slip. I got
in my auto, but I was startled to see them get
in their car. I headed for here, as I was coming to pay you a visit, anyhow, and the mysterious men kept after me. It became a regular race.
I put on all the speed I could and headed for
your house, Tom, for I thought you would help
me. I went faster and faster, and so did they.
They were almost up to me, and I was just thinking of slowing down to turn in here, when I lost
control of my machine, and—well, I did turn in
here, but not exactly as I intended. Bless my
gaiters! I came in with rather more of a rush

than I expected. It was awful—positively awful, I assure you. You've no idea how nervous I was. But I escaped those scoundrels, for they rushed on when they saw what I had done—smashed the porch railing."

"Probably they thought you'd smash them," observed Tom with a laugh. "But why did they follow you?"

"Can't imagine! Haven't the least idea. Bless my spark-plug, but they might have imagined I had money. Anyhow I'm glad I escaped them!"

"It's lucky you weren't hurt," said Mr. Sharp.

"Oh, me? Bless my existence! I'm always having narrow escapes." Mr. Damon caught sight of the *Red Cloud* which was out in front of the big shed. "Bless my heart! What's that?" he added.

"Our new airship," answered Tom proudly. "We are just planning a long trip in it, but we can't find a third member of the party to go along."

"A third member!" exclaimed Mr. Damon. "Do you really mean it?"

"We do."

"Bless my shoe laces! Will you take me along?"

"Do you mean that?" asked Tom in turn, fore-seeing a way out of their difficulties.

"I certainly do," answered the eccentric man. "I am much interested in airships, and I might as well die up in the clouds as any other way. Certainly I prefer it to being smashed up in an auto. Will you take me?"

"Of course!" cried Tom heartily, and Mr. Sharp nodded an assent. Then Tom drew Mr. Damon to one side. "We'll arrange the trip in a few minutes," the lad said. "Tell me more about those mysterious men, please."

CHAPTER X

A BAG OF TOOLS

WAKEFIELD DAMON glanced at Mr. Swift. The inventor was oblivious to his surroundings, and was busy figuring away on some paper. He seemed even to have forgotten the presence of the eccentric autoist.

"I don't want father to hear about the men," went on Tom, in a low tone. "If he hears that Happy Harry and his confederates are in this vicinity, he'll worry, and that doesn't agree with him. But are you sure the men you saw are the same ones who stole the turbine model?"

"Very certain," replied Mr. Damon. "I had a good view of them as I came from the bank, and I was surprised to see them, until I remembered that they were out of jail."

"But why do you think they pursued you?"

"Bless my eyes! I can't say. Perhaps they weren't after me at all. I may have imagined it, but they certainly hurried off in their auto as soon as I left the bank, after leaving my money there. I'm glad I deposited it before I saw them. I was so nervous, as it was, that I couldn't steer straight. It's too bad, the way I've damaged your house."

"That doesn't matter. But how about the trip in the airship? I hope you meant it when you said you would go."

"Of course I did. I've never traveled in the air, but it can't be much worse than my experience with my motor-cycle and the auto. At least I can't run up any stoop, can I?" and Mr. Damon looked at Mr. Sharp.

"No," replied the aeronaut, as he scratched his head, "I guess you'll be safe on that score. But I hope you won't get nervous when we reach a great height."

"Oh, no. I'll just calm myself with the reflection that I can't die but once," and with this philosophical reflection Mr. Damon went back to look at the auto, which certainly looked odd, stuck up on the veranda.

"Well, you'd better make arrangements to go with us then," went on Tom. "Meanwhile I'll see to getting your car down. You'll want to send it home, I suppose?"

"No, not if you'll keep it for me. The fact is that all my folks are away, and will be for

some time. I don't have to go home to notify
them, and it's a good thing, as my wife is very
nervous, and might object, if she heard about the
airship. I'll just stay here, if you've no objection,
until the *Red Cloud* sails, if sails is the proper
term."

" 'Sails' will do very well," answered Mr. Sharp.
"But, Tom, let's see if you and I can't get that
car down. Perhaps Mr. Damon would like to go
in the house and talk to your father," for Mr.
Swift had left the piazza.

The eccentric individual was glad enough not
to be on hand when his car was eased down from
the veranda and disappeared into the house. Tom
and Mr. Sharp, with the aid of Garret Jackson,
then released the auto from its position. They
had to take down the rest of the broken railing,
and their task was easy enough. The machine
was stored in a disused shed, and Mr. Damon
had no further concern until it was time to undertake the trip through the air.

"It will fool those men if I mysteriously disappear," he said, with a smile. "Bless my hat
band, but they'll wonder what became of me.
We'll just slip off in the *Red Cloud,* and they'll
never be the wiser."

"I don't know about that," commented Tom.
"I fancy they are keeping pretty close watch in

this vicinity, and I don't like it. I'm afraid they are up to some mischief. I should think the bank authorities would have them locked up on suspicion. I think I'll telephone Ned about it."

He did so, and his chum, in turn, notified the bank watchman. But the next day it was reported that no sign of the men had been seen, and, later it was learned that an auto, answering the description of the one they were in, had been seen going south, many miles from Shopton.

The work of preparing the *Red Cloud* for the long trip was all but completed. It had been placed back in the shed while a few more adjustments were made to the machinery.

"Bless my eyelashes!" exclaimed Mr. Damon, a few days before the one set for the start, "but I haven't asked where we are bound for. Where are we going, anyhow, Mr. Sharp?"

"We're going to try and reach Atlanta, Georgia," replied the balloonist. "That will make a fairly long trip, and the winds at this season are favorable in that direction."

"That suits me all right," declared Mr. Damon. "I'm all ready and anxious to start."

It was decided to give the airship a few more trials around Shopton before setting out, to see how it behaved with the car heavier loaded than usual. With this in view a trip was made to

Rocksmond, with Mr. Swift, Mr. Damon and Ned, in addition to Mr. Sharp and Tom, on board. Then, at Tom's somewhat blushing request, a stop was made near the Seminary, and, when the pupils came trooping out, the young inventor asked Miss Nestor if she didn't want to take a little flight. She consented, and with two pretty companions climbed rather hesitatingly into the car. No great height was attained, but the girls were fully satisfied and, after their first alarm really enjoyed the spin in the air, with Tom proudly presiding at the steering wheel, which Mr. Sharp relinquished to the lad, for he understood Tom's feelings.

Three days later all was in readiness for the trip to Atlanta. Mr. Swift was earnestly invited to undertake it, both Tom and Mr. Sharp urging him, but the veteran inventor said he must stay at home, and work on his submarine plans.

The evening before the start, when the aeronaut and Tom were giving a final inspection to the craft in the big shed, Mr. Sharp exclaimed:

"I declare Tom, I believe you'll have to take a run into town."

"What for?"

"Why to get that kit of special tools I ordered, which we might need to make repairs. There are some long-handled wrenches, some spare levers,

and a couple of braces and bits. Harrison, the
hardware dealer, ordered them for me from New
York, and they were to be ready this afternoon,
but I forgot them. Take an empty valise with
you, and you can carry them on your motor-
cycle. I'm sorry to have forgotten it, but—"

"That's all right, Mr. Sharp, I'd just as soon
go as not. It will make the time pass more
quickly. I'll start right off."

An hour later, having received the tools, which
made quite a bundle, the lad put them in the
valise, and started back toward home. As he
swung around the corner on which the bank was
located—the same bank in which Ned Newton
worked—one of the valves on the motor-cycle
began to leak. Tom dismounted to adjust it, and
had completed the work, being about to ride on,
when down the street came Andy Foger and Sam
Snedecker. They started at the sight of our
hero.

"There he is now!" exclaimed Sam, as if he
and the red-haired bully had been speaking of
the young inventor.

"Let's lick him!" proposed Andy. "Now's
our chance to get even for throwing that paint
and soot on us."

Tom heard their words. He was not afraid
of both the lads, for, though each one matched

him in size and strength, Tom knew they were cowards.

"If you're looking for anything I guess I can accommodate you," he said, coolly.

"Come on, Andy," urged Sam. But, somehow Andy hung back. Perhaps he didn't like the way Tom squared off. The young inventor had let down the rear brace of his motor-cycle, and was not obliged to hold it, so he had both hands free.

"We ought to lick him good and proper," growled the squint-eyed lad.

"Well, why don't you?" invited Tom.

He moved to one side, so as not to be hampered by his wheel. As he did so he knocked from the handle bars the valise of tools. They fell with a clatter and a thud to the pavement, and the satchel came open. It was under a gas lamp, and the glitter of the long-handled wrenches and other implements caught the eyes of Andy and his crony.

"Huh! If we fought you, maybe you'd use some of them on us," sneered Andy, glad of an excuse not to fight.

Tom quickly picked up his valise, shutting it, but he was aware of the close scrutiny of the two vindictive lads.

"I don't fight with such things," he said, somewhat annoyed, and he hung the tools back on the handle bars.

"What you doing around the bank at this hour?" asked Sam, as if to change the subject. "First thing you know the watchman will order you to move on. He might think you were a suspicious character."

"The same to you," retorted Tom, "but I'm going to ride on now, unless you want to have a further argument with me."

"You'd better be careful how you hang around a bank," added Andy. "The police are on the lookout here. There's been some mysterious men seen about."

Tom did not care to go into that, and, seeing that the two bullies had lost all desire to attack him, he put up the brace and mounted his wheel.

"Good-by," he called to Andy and Sam, as he rode off, the tools rattling and jingling in the valise, but it was a sarcastic farewell, and the two cronies did not reply.

"I hope I didn't damage any of the tools when I let them fall that time," mused the young inventor. "My, the way Sam and Andy stared at them it would make it seem as if I had a lot of weapons in the bag! They certainly took good note of them."

The time was to come, and very shortly, when

Andy's and Sam's observation of the tools **was** to prove disastrous for our hero. As Tom **turned the** corner he looked back, and saw, still **standing** in front of the bank, the two cronies.

CHAPTER XI

THE RED CLOUD DEPARTS

"WELL, dad, I wish you were going along with us," said Tom to his father next morning. "You don't know what you're going to miss. A fine trip of several hundred miles through the air, seeing strange sights, and experiencing new sensations."

"Yes, I wish you would reconsider your determination, and accompany us," added Mr. Damon. "I would enjoy your company."

"There's plenty of room. We can carry six persons with ease," said Mr. Sharp.

Mr. Swift shook his head, and smiled.

"I have too much work to do here at home," he replied. "Perhaps I may astonish you with something when you come back. I have nearly perfected my latest invention."

There was no combating such a resolution as this, and Tom and the others considered the decision of the aged inventor as final. The airship was ready for the start, and every one had arisen earlier than usual on this account. The bag of tools, for which Tom had gone to town, were put in their proper place, the last of the supplies were taken abroad, final tests were made of the various apparatus, the motor had been given a trial spin, disconnected from the propellers, and then the balloonist announced:

"Well, Tom and Mr. Damon, you had better begin to think of starting. We've had breakfast here, but there's no telling where we will eat dinner."

"Bless my soul! Don't you talk that way!" exclaimed Mr. Damon. "You make me exceed-ingly nervous. Why shouldn't we know where we are going to eat dinner?"

"Oh, I meant we couldn't tell over just what part of the United States we would be when din-ner time came," explained the aeronaut.

"Oh, that's different. Bless my pocket knife, but I thought you meant we might be dashed to pieces, and incapable of eating any dinner."

"Hardly," remarked Mr. Sharp. "The *Red Cloud* is not that kind of an airship, I hope. But get aboard, if you please."

Tom and Mr. Damon entered the car. It was resting on the ground, on the small wheels used to start the airship when the gas inflation method was not used. In this case, however, it had been decided to rise in the air by means of the powerful vapor, and not to use the wings and planes until another time. Consequently the ship was swaying slightly, and tugging at the restraining cables.

As Tom and Mr. Damon entered the cabin there drove into the Swift yard a dilapidated wagon, drawn by a bony mule, and it did not need the addition of a colored man's voice, calling: "Whoa, dar, Boomerang!" to tell Tom that his friend Eradicate Sampson was on hand. As for Eradicate, as soon as he saw the great airship, which he had never before beheld fully rigged, all ready for a flight, his eyes became big with wonder.

"Is dat yo' flyin' machine, Mistah Swift?" he asked.

"That's it, Rad," answered Tom. " Don't you want to come and take a ride with us?"

"Me? Good land a' massy! No indeedy, Mistah Swift," and the whitewasher, who had descended from his wagon, edged away, as if the airship might suddenly put out a pair of hands and grab him. "No indeedy I doant! I come t' do a little whitewashin' an' when I do dat I'se gwine on mah way. But dat's a pow'ful fine ship; it suah am!"

"Better come and try a flight, Rad," added **Mr.** Damon. "I'll look after you."

"No, sah, an' I doan't take it kind ob yo' all t' tempt me dat way, nuther," spoke Eradicate. But, when he saw that the craft was stationary, he ventured to approach closer. Gingerly he put out one hand and touched the framework of the wheels, just forward of the cabin. The negro grasped the timber, and lifted it slightly. To his astonishment the whole front of the airship tilted up, for it was about ready to fly, and a child might have lifted it, so buoyant was it. But Eradicate did not know this. Wonderingly he looked at the great bulk of the ship, looming above him, then he glanced at his arm. Once more, noting that the attention of his friends was elsewhere, he lifted the craft. Then he cried:

"Look yeah, Mistah Swift! Look yeah! No wonder day calls me Sampson. I done lifted dis monstrousness airship wif one hand. See, I kin do it! I kin do it!"

Once more he raised the *Red Cloud* slightly, and a delighted grin, not unmixed with a look of awe, spread over his honest countenance.

"I suppose you'll give up whitewashing and join a circus as a strong man, now," observed Mr. Sharp, with a wink at his companions.

"Dat's what I will!" announced Eradicate

proudly. "I neber knowed I was dat strong, but ob course I allers knowed I had some muscle. Golly, I must hab growed strong ober night! Now, Boomerang, yo' suah has got t' look out fo' yo' sef. No mo' ob yo' cuttin' up capers, or I'll jest lift you up, an' sot yo' down on yo' back, I suah will," and the negro feeling of his biceps walked over to where the mule stood, with its eyes closed.

"I guess you can cast off, Tom," called Mr. Sharp, as he entered the car, having seen that everything was all right. "We'll not go up very far at first, until Mr. Damon gets used to the thin air."

"Bless my soul, I believe I'm getting nervous," announced the eccentric man. "Bless my liver, but I hope nothing happens."

"Nothing will happen," Mr. Sharp assured him. "Just keep calm, when it feels as if the bottom was dropping out of everything and you'll soon get over it. Are you casting off those ropes, Tom? Is all clear?"

"All but the bow and stern lines."

"You attend to the bow line, and I'll go to the stern," and, going over to the gas generator, Mr. Sharp started it so as to force more vapor into the red aluminum container. This had the effect of rendering the airship more bouyant, and it tugged and strained harder than ever at the ropes.

"Good-by, Tom," called Mr. Swift, reaching up to shake hands with his son. "Drop me a line when you get a chance.

"Oh, Tom, do be careful," implored Mrs. Baggert, her kind face showing her anxiety. "May I kiss you good-by?"

"Of course," answered the young inventor, though the motherly housekeeper had not done this since he was a little chap. She had to stand on a soap box, which Eradicate brought in order to reach Tom's face, and, when she had kissed him she said:

"Oh, I'm so worried! I just know you'll be killed, risking your lives in that terrible airship!"

"Ha! Not a very cheerful view to take, madam," observed Mr. Damon. "Don't hold that view, I beg of you. Bless my eyelashes, but you'll see us coming home, covered with glory and star dust."

"I'm sure I hope so," answered Mrs. Baggert, laughing a little in spite of herself.

The last ropes were cast off. Good-bys were shouted as the airship shot into the air, and Mr. Sharp started the motor, to warm it up before the propellers were thrown into gear. The twenty cylinders began exploding with a terrific racket, as the muffler was open, and Tom, looking down, saw Boomerang awaken with a jump. The mule was so frightened that he started off on a dead run, swinging the rickety, old wagon along behind him.

Eradicate Sampson, who had been feeling his muscle since he discovered what he thought was his marvelous strength, saw what was happening.

"Whoa, dar, Boomerang!" he shouted. Then, as the tailboard of the wagon swung past him, he reached out and grabbed it. Perhaps he thought he could bring the runaway mule up standing, but, if he did, he was grievously disappointed. Boomerang pulled his master along the gravel walk, and kept running in spite of Eradicate's command to "whoa, dar!"

It might have gone hard with him, had not Garret Jackson, the engineer, running in front of Boomerang, caught the animal. Eradicate picked himself up, and gazed sadly at his arms. The navigators of the air could not hear what he said, but what he thought was evident to them.

Then, as Mr. Sharp deadened the explosions of the powerful motor. Tom, looking at a gauge, noted that their height was seven hundred feet.

"High enough!" called Mr. Sharp, and it was time, for Mr. Damon, in spite of his resolution, was getting pale.

The gas was shut off, the propellers thrown into gear, and, with a rush the *Red Cloud* shot toward the south, passing over the Swift homestead, and high above the heads of the crowd that had gathered to witness the start. The eventful voyage of the air had begun.

CHAPTER XII

SOME STARTLING NEWS

"WELL, there they go," remarked Mrs. Baggert to Mr. Swift, as she strained her eyes toward the sky, against the blue of which the airship was now only a large, black ball.

"Yes, and a fine start they made," replied the inventor. "I almost wish I had accompanied them, but I must not stop work on my submarine invention."

"I do hope nothing will happen to them," went on the housekeeper. I declare, though, I feel just as if something *was* going to happen."

"Nervousness, pure nervousness," commented Mr. Swift. "Better take a little—er—I suppose catnip tea would be good."

"Catnip tea! The very idea!" exclaimed Mrs. Baggert. "That shows how much you know about nervousness, Mr. Swift," and she seemed a little indignant.

"Ha! Hum! Well, maybe catnip tea wouldn't

be just the thing. But don't worry about Tom. I'm sure he can look after himself. As for Mr. Sharp he has made too many ascensions to run into any unnecessary danger."

"Nervous!" went on the housekeeper, who seemed to resent this state being applied to her. "I'm sure I'm not half as nervous as that Mr. Damon. He gives me the fidgets."

"Of course. Well, I must get back to my work," said the inventor. "Ah, are you hurt, Eradicate?" he went on, as the colored man came back, driving Boomerang, who had been stopped just before reaching the road.

"No, Mistah Swift, I ain't exactly damaged, but mah feelin's am suah hurted."

"How's that?"

"Well, I thought I had growed strong in de night, when I lifted dat airship, but when I went to stop mah mule I couldn't do it. He won't hab no respect fo' me now."

"Oh, I wouldn't let that worry me," commented Mr. Swift, and he explained to Eradicate how it was that he had so easily lifted the end of the bouyant ship, which weighed very little when filled with gas.

The colored man proceeded with his work of whitewashing, the inventor was in his library, puzzling over tables of intricate figures, and Mrs.

Baggert was in the kitchen, sighing occasionally as she thought of Tom, whom she loved almost as a son, high in the air, when two men came up the walk, from the street, and knocked at the side door. Mrs. Baggert, who answered the summons, was somewhat surprised to see Chief of Police Simonson and Constable Higby.

"They probably came to see the airship start," she thought, "but they're too late."

"Ah, good morning, Mrs. Baggert," greeted the chief. "Is Mr. Swift and his son about this morning?"

"Mr. Swift is in his library, but Tom is gone."

"He'll be back though, won't he?" asked Constable Higby quickly—anxiously, Mrs. Baggert thought.

"Oh, yes," she replied. "He and—"

"Just take us to see Mr. Swift," interrupted the chief, with a look of caution at his aide. "We'll explain matters to him."

Wondering what could be the mission of the two officers, Mrs. Baggert led them to the library.

"It's queer," she thought, "that they don't ask something about the airship. I suppose that was what they came for. But maybe it's about the mysterious men who robbed Mr. Swift."

"Ah, gentlemen, what can I do for you?" asked the inventor, as he rose to greet the officials.

"Ahem, Mr. Swift. Ahem—er—that is—well, the fact is, Mr. Swift," stammered the chief, "we have come upon a very painful errand."

"What's that?" cried Tom's father. "I haven't been robbed again, have I?"

"There has been a robbery committed," spoke the constable quickly.

"But you are not the victim," interposed the chief.

"I'm glad of that," said Mr. Swift.

"Where is your son, Tom?" asked the head of the Shopton police force, sharply.

"What do you want with him?" inquired the inventor, struck by some strange tone in the other's voice.

"Mr. Swift," went on the chief, solemnly, "I said we came upon a very painful errand. It is painful, as I have known Tom since he was a little lad. But I must do my duty, no matter how painful it is. I have a warrant for the arrest of your son, Thomas Swift, and I have come to serve it. I need not tell you that it is your duty to give him up to us—the representatives of the law. I call upon you to produce your son."

Mr. Swift staggered to his feet.

"My son! You have come to arrest my son?" he stammered.

The chief nodded grimly.

"Upon what charge?" faltered the father.

"On a charge of breaking into the Shopton National Bank last night, and stealing from the vault seventy-five thousand dollars in currency!"

"Seventy-five thousand dollars! Tom accused of robbing the bank!" faltered Mr. Swift.

"That is the charge, and we've come to arrest him," broke in Constable Higby.

"Where is he?" added the chief.

"This charge is false! Absolutely false!" shouted the aged inventor.

"That may be," admitted the chief shaking his head. "But the charge has been made, and we hold the warrant. The courts will settle it. We must now arrest Tom. Where is he?"

"He isn't here!" cried Mr. Swift, and small blame to him if there was a note of triumph in his voice. "Tom sailed away not half an hour ago in the airship *Red Cloud!* You can't arrest him!"

"He's escaped!" shouted the constable. "I told you, chief, that he was a slippery customer, and that we'd better come before breakfast!"

"Dry up!" commanded the chief testily. "So he's foiled us, eh? Run away when he knew we were coming? I think that looks like guilt, Mr. Swift."

"Never!" cried the inventor. "Tom would never think of robbing the bank. Besides, he has all the money he wants. The charge is preposterous! I demand to be confronted with the proof."

"You shall be," answered Chief Simonson vindictively. "If you will come to the bank you can see the rifled vault, and hear the testimony of a witness who saw your son with burglar tools in his possession last night. We also have a warrant for Mr. Wakefield Damon. Do you know anything of him?"

"He has gone with my son in the airship."

"Ha! The two criminals with their booty have escaped together!" cried the chief. "But we'll nab them if we have to scour the whole country. Come on, Higby! Mr. Swift, if you'll accompany me to the bank, I think I can give you all the proof you want," and the officials, followed by the amazed and grief-stricken inventor, left the house.

CHAPTER XIII

MR. DAMON IN DANGER

THE sensations of the voyagers in the airship, who meanwhile, were flying along over the country surrounding Shopton, were not very different than when they had undertaken some trial flights. In fact Mr. Damon was a little disappointed after they had waved their farewells to Mr. Swift and Mrs. Baggert.

"I declare I'm not at all nervous," he remarked, as he sat in an easy chair in the enclosed car or cabin, and looked down at the earth through the plate-glass windows in the floor.

"I thought you'd be all right once we got started," commented Mr. Sharp. "Do you think you can stand going a trifle higher?"

"Try it," suggested the eccentric man. "Bless my watch chain, but, as I said, I might as well die this way as any other. Hitting a cloud-bank is easier than trying to climb a tree on a motor-cycle, eh, Tom?"

"Very much so, Mr. Damon," conceded the young inventor, with a laugh.

"Oh, we'll not attempt any cloud heights for a day or two," went on Mr. Sharp. "I want you to gradually get used to the rarefied atmosphere, Mr. Damon. Tom and I are getting to be old hands at it. But, if you think you can stand it, I'll go up about a thousand feet higher."

"Make it two thousand, while you're at it," proposed the odd character. "Might as well take a long fall as a short one."

Accordingly, the elevation rudder was used to send the *Red Cloud* to a greater height while she was still skimming along like some great bird. Of course the desired elevation could have been obtained by forcing more gas from the machine into the big, red container overhead, but it was decided to be as sparing of this vapor as possible, since the voyagers did not want to descend to get more material, in case they used up what they had. It was just as easy to rise by properly working the rudders, when the ship was in motion, and that was the method now employed.

With the great propellers, fore and aft, making about a thousand revolutions a minute the craft slanted up toward the sky.

The ship was not being run at top speed as Mr. Sharp did not care to force it, and there was no need for haste. Long distance, rather than high speed was being aimed at on this first important flight.

Tom was at the steering wheel, and, with his hand on the lever controlling the elevation rudder, kept watch of the face of Mr. Damon, occasionally noting what height the hand on the gauge registered. He fancied he saw the cheeks of his friend growing pale, and, when a height of thirty-five hundred feet was indicated, with a yank the young inventor put the airship on a level keel.

"Are you distressed, Mr. Damon?" he asked.

"Ye—yes, I—I have—some—some difficulty in breathing," was the answer.

Tom gave his friend the same advice the aeronaut had given the lad on his first trip, and the eccentric man soon felt better.

"Bless my buttons!" he ventured to explain. "But I feel as if I had lost several pounds of flesh, and I'm glad of it."

Mr. Sharp was busy with the motor, which needed some slight adjustments, and Tom was in sole charge of navigating the airship. He had lost the nervous feeling that first possessed him, and was beccoming quite an expert at meeting various currents of wind encountered in the upper regions.

Below, the voyagers could see the earth spread

out like a great map. They could not tell their exact location now, but by calculating their speed, which was about thirty miles an hour, Tom figured out that they were above the town of Centreford, near where he had been attacked once by the model thieves.

For several hours the airship kept on her way, maintaining a height of about a mile, for when it was found that Mr. Damon could accommodate himself to thirty-five hundred feet the elevation rudder was again shifted to send the craft upward.

By using glasses the travelers could see crowds on the earth watching their progress in the air, and, though airships, dirigible balloons and aeroplanes are getting fairly common now, the appearance of one as novel and as large as the *Red Cloud* could always be depended upon to attract attention.

"Well, what do you say to something to eat?" proposed Mr. Sharp, coming into the main cabin, from the motor compartment. "It's twelve o'clock, though we can't hear the factory whistles up here."

"I'm ready, any time you are," called Tom, from the pilot house. "Shall I cook grub, Mr. Sharp?"

"No, you manage the ship, and I'll play cook.

We'll not get a very elaborate meal this time, as I shall have to pay occasional visits to the motor, which isn't running just to suit me."

The electrical stove was set going, and some soup and beefsteak from among the stores, was put on the fire. In spite of the fact that the day was a warm one in October, it was quite cool in the cabin, until the stove took off the chill. The temperature of the upper regions was several degrees below that of the earth. At times the ship passed through little wisps of vapor-clouds in the making.

"Isn't this wonderful!" exclaimed Mr. Damon, as he sat in an easy chair, partaking of some of the food. "To think that I have lived to see the day when I can take my lunch a mile in the air, with a craft flying along like a bird. Bless my knife and fork but it certainly is wonderful!"

Mr. Sharp relieved Tom at the wheel, while the young inventor ate, and then, with the air-ship heading southwest, the speed was increased a trifle, the balloonist desiring to see what the motor could accomplish under a heavy load.

A drop of several hundred feet was made about an hour later, and, as this made it warmer, Mr. Damon, who was a great lover of fresh air, decided to go out on the platform in front of the cabin. This platform, and a similar one at the rear, was railed about, to prevent accidents. A fine view could be had from them much better than through the floor windows of the car.

"Be careful of the propeller," advised Tom, as his friend went outside. "I don't believe you're tall enough to be hit by the blades, but don't take any chances of standing on your tiptoes."

"Bless my pocket handkerchief, indeed I'll not," came the answer. "But I think I shall wrap up my throat in the scarf I brought along. I am subject to neuralgia, and the breeze may bring on an attack of it."

Wrapping a long, woolen scarf about his neck, the eccentric man ventured out on the open platform. About the middle of it, but sufficiently high to be above a person's head, was the forward propeller, whirring around at swift speed.

Tom, with his eye on the various gauges and the compass, was steering the airship. He glanced at Mr. Damon, who appeared to be enjoying the view from the platform. For an instant the eyes of the lad were taken from the form of his friend. He looked back suddenly, however, his attention attracted by a smothered cry. He was horrified by what he saw.

Mr. Damon was leaning far over the edge of the railing, with nothing between him and the earth a thousand feet below. He seemed to have lost his balance and had toppled forward, being doubled up on the iron pipe railing, his hands hanging limply over. Then, as Tom cried to Mr. Sharp to shut off the motor, the lad saw that hanging to the blade of the propeller, and being whirled around in its revolutions, was a part of Mr. Damon's red scarf.

"Hurry! Hurry, Mr. Sharp!" yelled Tom, not daring to let go the steering wheel, for fear the ship would encounter a treacherous current and tilt. "Hurry to Mr. Damon!"

"What's the matter?" asked the balloonist.

"He's dead—or unconscious—hanging over the railing. He seems to be slipping! Hurry, or it will be too late!"

CHAPTER XIV

ANDY GIVES THE CLUE

When Mr. Swift followed the chief of police and the constable to the town hall his mind was filled with many thoughts. All his plans for revolutionizing submarine travel, were, of course, forgotten, and he was only concerned with the charge that had been made against his son. It seemed incredible, yet the officers were not ones to perpetrate a joke. The chief and constable had driven from town in a carriage, and they now invited the inventor to ride back with them.

"Do you mean to tell me a warrant has actually been sworn out against my son, Chief?" asked the father, when they were near the town hall.

"That's just what I mean to say, Mr. Swift, and I'm sorry, on your account, that I have to serve it."

"Huh! Don't look like you was goin' to serve it," remarked the constable. "He's skipped out."

"That's all right, Higby," went on the chief.

"I'll catch em both. Even if they have escaped in an airship with their booty, I'll nab 'em. I'll have a general alarm out all over the country in less than an hour. They can't stay up in the air forever."

"A warrant for Tom—my son," murmured Mr. Swift, as if he could not believe it.

"Yes, and for that Damon man, too," added the chief. "I want him as well as Tom, and I'll get 'em."

"Would you mind letting me see the warrants?" asked the inventor, and the official passed them over. The documents were made out in regular form, and the complaints had been sworn to by Isaac Pendergast, the bank president.

"I can't understand it," went on Tom's father. "Seventy-five thousand dollars. It's incredible! Why!" he suddenly exclaimed, "it can't be true. Just before he left, Mr. Damon——"

"Yes, what did he do?" asked the chief eagerly, thinking he might secure some valuable evidence.

"I guess I'll say nothing until I have seen the bank president," replied Mr. Swift, and the official was obviously disappointed.

The inventor found Mr. Pendergast, and some other bank officials in the town hall. The financiers were rather angry when they learned that the accused persons had not been caught, but the chief said he would soon have them in custody.

"In the meanwhile will you kindly explain what this means?" asked Mr. Swift of the president.

"You may come and look at the looted vault, if you like, Mr. Swift," replied Mr. Pendergast. "It was a very thorough job, and will seriously cripple the bank."

There was no doubt that the vault had been forced open, for the locks and bars were bent and twisted as if by heavy tools. Mr. Swift made a careful examination, and was shown the money drawers that had been smashed.

"This was the work of experts," he declared.

"Exactly what we think," said the president. "Of course we don't believe your son was a professional bank robber, Mr. Swift. We have a theory that Mr. Damon did the real work, but that Tom helped him with the tools he had. There is no doubt about it."

"What right have you to accuse my son?" burst out the aged inventor. "Why have you any more cause to suspect him than any other lad in town? Why do you fix on him, and Mr. Damon? I demand to know."

"Mr. Damon's eccentric actions for a few days past, and his well-known oddity of character make him an object of suspicion," declared the president in judicial tones. "As for Tom, we have, I regret to say, even better evidence against him."

"But what is it? What? Who gave you any clues to point to my son?"

"Do you really wish to know?"

"I certainly do," was the sharp reply. Mr. Swift, the police and several bank officials were now in the president's office. The latter pressed an electric bell, and, when a messenger answered, he said:

"Send young Foger here."

At the mention of this name, Mr. Swift started. He well knew the red-haired bully was an enemy of his son. Andy entered, walking rather proudly at the attention he attracted.

"This is Mr. Swift," said the president.

"Aw, I know him," blurted out Andy.

"You will please tell him what you told us," went on Mr. Pendergast.

"Well, I seen Tom Swift hanging around this bank with burglar tools in his possession last night, just before it was robbed," exclaimed the squint-eyed lad triumphantly.

"Hanging around the bank last night with burglar tools?" repeated Mr. Swift, in dazed tones.

"That's right," from Andy.

"How do you know they were burglar tools?"

"Because I saw 'em!" cried Andy. "He had 'em in a valise on his motor-cycle. He was standing at the corner, waiting for a chance to break into the bank, and when me and Sam Snedecker saw him, he pretended to be fixin' his machine. Then the bag of burglar tools fell off, the satchel came open, and I seen 'em! That's how I know."

"And you're sure they were burglar tools?" asked the chief, for he depended on Andy to be his most important witness.

"Sure I am. I seen a picture of burglar tools once, and the ones Tom had was just like 'em. Long-handled wrenches, brace an' bits, an' all. He tried to hide 'em, but me an' Sam was too quick for him. He wanted to lick me, too."

"No doubt you deserved it," murmured Mr. Swift. "But how do you know my son was waiting for a chance to break into the bank?"

" 'Cause, wasn't it robbed right after he was hangin' around here with the burglar tools?" inquired Andy, as if that was unanswerable.

"What were you hanging around here for?" Mr. Swift demanded quickly.

"Me? Oh, well, me an' Sam Snedecker was out takin' a walk. That's all."

"You didn't want to rob the bank, did you?" went on the inventor, keenly.

"Of course not," roared the bully, indignantly. "I ain't got no burglar tools."

Andy told more along the same line, but his testimony of having seen Tom near the bank, with a bag of odd tools could not be shaken. In fact it was true, as far as it went, but, of course, the tools were only those for the airship; the same ones Mr. Sharp had sent the lad after. Sam Snedecker was called in after Andy, and told substantially the same story.

Mr. Swift could not understand it, for he knew nothing of Tom being sent for the tools, and had not heard any talk at home of the bag of implements ordered by the balloonist. Still, of course, he knew Tom had nothing to do with the robbery, and he knew his son had been at home all the night previous. Still this was rather negative evidence. But the inventor had one question yet to ask.

"You say you also suspect Mr. Damon of complicity in this affair?" he went on, to the chief of police.

"We sure do," replied Mr. Simonson.

"Then can you explain?" proceeded the inventor, "how it is that Mr. Damon has on deposit in this bank a large sum. Would he rob the bank where his own funds were?"

"We are prepared for that," declared the

president. "It is true that Mr. Damon has about ten thousand dollars in our bank, but we believe he deposited it only as a blind, so as to cover up his tracks. It is a deep-laid scheme, and escaping in the airship is part of it. I am sorry, Mr. Swift, that I have to believe your son and his accomplice guilty, but I am obliged to. Chief, you had better send out a general alarm. The airship ought to be easy to trace."

"I'll telegraph at once," said the official.

"And you believe my son guilty, solely on the testimony of these two boys, who, as is well known, are his enemies?" asked Mr. Swift.

"The clue they gave us is certainly most important," said the president. "Andy came to us and told what he had seen, as soon as it became known that the bank had been robbed."

"And I'm going to get the reward for giving information of the robbers, too!" cried the bully.

"I'm going to have my share!" insisted Sam.

"Ah, then there is a reward offered?" inquired Mr. Swift.

"Five thousand dollars," answered Mr. Pendergast. "The directors, all of whom are present save Mr. Foger, Andy's father, met early this morning, and decided to offer that sum."

"And I'm going to get it," announced the red-haired lad again.

Mr. Swift was much downcast. There seemed to be nothing more to say, and, being a man unversed in the ways of the world, he did not know what to do. He returned home. When Mrs. Baggert was made acquainted with the news, she waxed indignant.

"Our Tom a thief!" she cried. "Why don't they accuse me and Mr. Jackson and you? The idea! You ought to hire a lawyer, Mr. Swift, and prosecute those men for slander."

"Do you think it would be a good plan?"

"I certainly do. Why they have no evidence at all! What does that mean, sneaking Andy Foger amount to? Get a lawyer, and have Tom's interests looked after."

Mr. Swift, glad to have some one share the responsibility with, felt somewhat better when a well-known Shopton attorney assured him that the evidence against Tom was of such a flimsy character that it would scarcely hold in a court of justice.

"But they have warrants for him and Mr. Damon," declared the inventor.

"Very true, but it is easy to swear out a warrant against any one. It's a different matter to prove a person guilty."

"But they can arrest my son."

"Yes—if they catch him. However, we can soon have him released on bail."

"It's disgraceful," said Mrs. Baggert.

"Not at all, my dear madam, not at all. Good and innocent persons have been arrested."

"They are going to send out a general alarm for my son," bewailed Mr. Swift.

"Yes, but I fancy it will be some time before they catch him and Mr. Damon, if the airship holds together. I can't think of a better way to keep out of the clutches of the police, and their silly charge," chuckled the lawyer. "Now don't worry, Mr. Swift. It will all come out right.

The inventor tried to believe so, but, though he knew his son was innocent, it was rather hard to see, within the next few days, big posters on all the vacant walls and fences, offering a reward of five thousand dollars for the arrest of Tom Swift and Wakefield Damon, who were charged with having flown away in an airship with seventy-five thousand dollars of the bank's money.

"I guess Tom Swift will wish he'd been more decent to me when I collect that money for his arrest," said Andy to his crony, Sam, the day the bills were posted.

"Yes, but I get my share, don't I?" asked Sam.

"Sure," answered the bully. "I wish they'd hurry up and arrest him."

Within the next few days the country was covered with posters telling of the robbery and the reward, and police officials in cities large and small, and in towns and villages, were notified by telegraph to arrest and capture, at any cost the occupants of a certain large, red airship.

Mr. Swift, on the advice of his lawyer, sent several telegrams to Tom, apprising him of what had happened. The telegraph company was asked to rush the telegrams to the first city when word came in that the *Red Cloud* had landed.

CHAPTER XV

FIRED UPON

TOM's excited call to the aeronaut, telling of the mishap to Mr. Damon, was answered immediately. Mr. Sharp jumped forward from the motor compartment, and, passing on his way the electric switch, he yanked it out, stopping the machinery, and the great propellers. Then he leaped out on the platform.

But something else happened. Just before the accident to the eccentric man, desiring to give a further test to the planes, the gas had been shut off, making the airship an aeroplane instead of a dirigible balloon. Consequently, as soon as the forward motion ceased the great ship began falling.

"We're sinking! We're sinking!" cried Tom, forgetting for a moment that he was not in his motor-boat.

"Slant your rudder up, and glide downward as slowly as you can!" directed Mr. Sharp. "I'll start the engine again as soon as I rescue him," for it was risky to venture out on the platform with the propeller whirring, as the dangling piece of scarf might whip around the balloonist and toss him off.

Mr. Sharp was soon at Mr. Damon's side. He saw that the man was unconscious, whether from fright or some injury could not then be determined. There was, however, no sign of a wound.

It was no easy task to carry, half dragging it, the heavy body of Mr. Damon off the platform, but the aeronaut was a muscular individual, and long hanging from a trapeze, at great heights, stood him in good stead.

He brought the unconscious man into the cabin, and then, quickly returning to the platform, he detached the piece of scarf from the propeller blade. Next he started the motor, and also turned on the gas tank, so that the airship, in a few minutes, could float in space without motion.

"You needn't steer now, Tom," said the balloonist. "Just give me a hand here."

"Is—is he dead?" inquired the lad, his voice faltering.

"No, his heart's beating. I can't understand what happened."

Mr. Sharp was something of a rough and ready surgeon and doctor, and a small box of medicines had been brought along in case of emergencies. With the *Red Cloud* now lazily floating in the air, for, once the falling motion had been checked by the engine, the motor had been stopped again, Mr. Sharp set about restoring Mr. Damon to consciousness.

It was not long before the man opened his eyes. The color that had left his cheeks came back, and, after a drink of cold water he was able to sit up.

"Did I fall?" he asked. "Bless my very existence, but did I tumble off the airship?"

"No indeed," replied Tom, "though you came pretty near it. How do you feel? Were you hurt?"

"Oh, I'm all right now—just a trifle dizzy. But I thought sure I was a goner when I fell over the platform railing," and Mr. Damon could not repress a shudder. Mr. Sharp administered some more medicine and his patient was soon able to stand, and move about.

"How did it happen?" inquired the balloonist.

"I hardly know," answered Mr. Damon. "I was out on the platform, looking at the view, and thinking how much better my neuralgia was, with the scarf on. Suddenly the wind whipped loose one end of the scarf, and, before I knew it the cloth had caught on the propeller blade. I was blown, or drawn to one side, tossed against the railing, which I managed to grab, and then I lost my senses. It's a good thing I wasn't whirled around the propeller."

"It's a good thing you weren't tossed down to the earth," commented Tom, shivering as he thought of his friend's narrow escape.

"I became unconscious, partly because the wind was knocked from me as I hit the platform railing," went on Mr. Damon, "and partly from fright, I think. But I'm all right now, and I'm not going out on that platform again with a loose scarf on."

"I wouldn't go out at all again, if I were you, though, of course, I'm used to dizzy heights," spoke Mr. Sharp.

"Oh, I'm not so easily frightened," declared Mr. Damon. "If I'm going to be a balloonist, or an aeroplanist I've got to get used to certain things. I'm all right now," and the plucky man was, for the blow to his side did not amount to much. It was some time, however, before Tom got over the fright his friend had caused him.

They spent that night moving slowly south, and in the morning found they had covered about a hundred miles, not having run the ship to anything like its maximum speed. Breakfast was served above the clouds, for a change, Mr. Damon finding that he could stand the great height with comfort.

It was three days after the start, and the travelers were proceeding slowly along. They were totally unaware, of course, of the sensation which their leaving, conjointly with the bank robbery, had caused, not only in Shopton but in other places.

"We're over a good-sized city," announced Tom, on the noon of the third day. "Suppose we drop down, and leave some message? Dad will be anxious to hear from us."

"Good idea," commented Mr. Sharp. "Down it is. Shift the rudder."

Tom proceeded to do so, and, while Mr. Damon relieved him at the wheel the young inventor prepared a message to his father. It was placed in a weighted envelope, together with a sum of money, and the person picking it up was requested to send the letter as a telegram, retaining some money for his trouble.

As the ship got lower and lower over the city the usual crowds could be seen congregating in the streets, pointing and gazing upward.

"We're creating quite a stir," observed Tom.

"More than usual, it seems," added Mr. Sharp, peering down. "I declare, there seems to be a police parade under way."

"That's right," put in Mr. Damon, for, looking down, a squad of uniformed officers, some on horseback, could be seen hurrying along the main street, trying to keep pace with the airship, which was moving slowly.

"They're looking at us through telescopes," called Tom. "Guess they never saw a balloon down this way."

Nearer and nearer to the city dropped the *Red Cloud*. Tom was about to let go the weighted envelope, when, from the midst of the police came several puffs of white smoke. It was followed by vicious, zipping sounds about the cabin of the ship, the windows of which were open. Then came the reports of several rifles.

"They're firing at us!" yelled Tom.

"So they are!" cried Mr. Sharp. "They must be crazy! Can't they see that we're not a bird."

"Maybe they take us for a war balloon," suggested Mr. Damon.

Another volley was directed at the airship, and several bullets struck the big aluminum gas holder glancing blows.

"Here! Quit that!" yelled Tom, leaning out of the window. "Are you crazy? You'll damage us!"

"They can't hear you," called Mr. Sharp.

A third volley was fired, and this time several

persons other than police officers seemed to be shooting at the airship. Revolvers as well as rifles were being used.

"We're got to get out of this!" shouted Mr. Sharp, as a bullet sang uncomfortably close to his head. "I can't imagine what's gotten into the people. Send her up, Tom!"

The lad quickly shifted the elevation rudder, and the *Red Cloud* sailed majestically aloft. The young inventor had not dropped his message, concluding that citizens who would fire on travelers of the air for no reason, would not be likely to accommodate them in the matter of sending messages.

The craft mounted rapidly upward, but before it was beyond rifle shot another volley was fired, one bullet sending some splinters flying from the wooden framework.

"Whew! That was a narrow escape!" exclaimed Mr. Sharp. "What in the world can those people be up to, anyhow?"

CHAPTER XVI

OVER A FIERY FURNACE

Down below, the aeronauts could see the crowd, led by the police, scurrying to and fro. Many individuals beside the officers appeared to be holding weapons, and, from the puffs of smoke that spurted out, it was evident that more shots were being fired. But the bullets could do no harm, and the *Red Cloud*, under the force of the rapidly revolving propellers, was soon beyond the center of the city.

"Well, if that isn't the limit!" cried Tom. "They must have taken us for a German war balloon, about to drop explosives on them."

"Bless my liver!" ejaculated Mr. Damon, "I believe you're right. Eh, Mr. Sharp?"

The veteran balloonist took a careful look over the craft before replying. Then he spoke:

"It couldn't be that," and he shook his head, as if puzzled. "They would know no foreign airship would try any trick like that. Beside, if by some remote possibility they did imagine it, there would be soldiers shooting at us, instead of the police.   As it was, the whole population seemed anxious to bring us down."

"And they nearly did," added Mr. Damon.   "If they had shot a few holes in the gas bag where would we be?"

"Right in the air," answered the balloonist. "It would take several volleys of bullets to damage our aluminum container.   It is in sections and when one, or even five compartments, for that matter, are pierced, there is enough gas in the others to sustain us.   So they could not have damaged us much, even if they had shot a lot of holes in us.   Even without the gas container we can keep afloat by constantly moving, for the planes will serve their purpose.   Of course they could damage us, and maybe put some of our machinery out of business, and that would be a serious thing.   But what puzzles me is why they fired at us at all."

"It couldn't be out of pure mischief; could it?" asked the young inventor.

"Hardly.   If we were in a savage country I could understand the natives firing at some such object as this airship, but the people of that city must have known what our craft was.   They probably have read something about it in the newspapers, and to deliberately fire on us, with the chance of disabling us, seems worse than barbarous."

"Well, we won't give 'em another opportunity," commented Mr. Damon.

"No, indeed, not this city, but who knows but what the example may spread? We may be fired at the next town we sail over."

"Then steer clear of the towns," advised Tom.

"Impossible. We must pass over some, but I'd like to solve this mystery."

The day passed without further incident, though they did not go low enough down over any city to drop any messages. It was decided that it would not be safe.

"We'll take a chance at night," suggested Tom, and that evening, approaching a good-sized town in the dusk, several of the weighted envelopes were dropped overboard. Doubtless persons walking along the street, who were startled by hearing something fall with a "thud" at their feet, were much startled to look up and see, dimly, a great, ghostly shape moving in the air. But there was no shooting, and, eventually, some of the messages reached Mr. Swift, in Shopton. But he could not answer them for the airship kept on the move.

The night was spent floating in the air, with the

engine stopped, and the *Red Cloud* floating lazily this way and that as the gentle winds shifted, for it was calm. The "anchorage" if such it may be called, was above a sparsely settled part of the country, and if the lights of the airship were seen from below, the farmers doubtless took them for some new stars or, possibly, a comet.

"Now then for a fast, straight run!" cried Tom, after breakfast had been served, and the big motor, with its twenty cylinders, started. "We'll be able to make the turn to-day, and then make for home, won't we, Mr. Sharp?"

"Well, we could do it, Tom," was the answer, "but I like this mode of traveling so that I think I'll lengthen the voyage. Instead of turning at Atlanta, what do you say to making for Key West, and then starting back? That will be something of a trip. The *Red Cloud* is behaving much better than I hoped she would."

"I'm willing to go further if Mr. Damon is."

"Oh, bless my shoe strings, I'm game!" exclaimed the eccentric man. "I always did want to go to Key West, anyhow."

The craft was speeding along at a fast clip, and dinner that day was served about three miles in the air. Then, desiring to test the gliding abilities of the airship, it was sent down on a long slant, with the propellers stationary, the shifting planes and rudders alone guiding it.

As the craft fairly slid down out of the sky, like a sled on a bank of fleecy snow, Tom, who was peering ahead, with his hand on the steering wheel, cried out:

"I say! It looks as if we were going to run into a thunder storm!"

"How's that?" inquired Mr. Sharp, poking his head from the motor compartment.

"He says there's a big storm ahead," repeated Mr. Damon, "and I guess he's right. I see a big bank of dark clouds, and there is a roaring in the air."

Mr. Sharp, who had been making some adjustments to the motor went forward to take a look. The *Red Cloud* was swiftly gliding downward on a slant, straight toward a dark mass of vapor, that seemed to be rolling first one way, and then another, while as Mr. Damon had said, there was a low rumbling proceeding from it.

"That doesn't seem to be a thunder storm," spoke the balloonist, with a puzzled air.

They all regarded the dark mass of vapor intently for a few seconds. Tom had brought the airship to a more level keel, and it was now spinning along under its own momentum, like a flat piece of tin, scaled by some lead. But it was headed for the clouds, if such they were, though losing speed by degrees.

"I'll have to start the motor!" exclaimed Mr. Sharp. "We don't want to run into a storm, if we can help it, though I don't ever remember seeing a thunder disturbance like that."

"Whew! It's getting warm," suddenly announced the youth, and he let go of the steering wheel for a moment, while he took off his coat.

"That's what it is," agreed Mr. Damon, who also divested himself of his garments. "Bless my spark plug, but it's like a July day. No wonder there's a thunderstorm ahead."

Then Mr. Sharp uttered a cry.

"That's no storm!" he fairly shouted. "It's a big forest fire! That's smoke we see! We must get out of this. Turn around Tom, while I start the engine. We must rise above it!"

He fairly leaped for the motor, and Tom and Mr. Damon could hear him turning the levers and wheels, ready to start. But before the explosions came something happened. There was a sound as of some great, siren whistle blowing, and then, with a howl of the on rushing air, the *Red Cloud*, the propellers of which hung motionless on their shafts, was fairly sucked forward toward the fire, as the current sucks a boat over a water fall.

"Start the motor! Start the motor, Mr. Sharp!" cried Tom.

"I'm trying to, but something seems to be the matter."

"We're being drawn right over the fire!" yelled Mr. Damon. "It's getting hotter every minute! Can't you do something?"

"You take the wheel," called the balloonist to Mr. Damon. "Steer around, just as if it was an auto when we start the engine. Tom, come here and give me a hand. The motor has jammed!"

The young inventor sprang to obey. Mr. Damon, his face showing some of the fear he felt, grasped the steering wheel. The airship was now about a quarter of a mile high, but instead of resting motionless in the air, sustained by the gas in the container, she was being pulled forward, right toward the heart of the mass of black vapor, which it could now be seen was streaked with bright tongues of flame.

"What's making us go ahead, if the motor isn't going?" asked Tom, as he bent over the machine, at which the aeronaut was laboring.

"Suction—draught from the fire!" explained Mr. Sharp. "Heated air rises and leaves a vacuum. The cold air rushes in. It's carrying us with it. We'll be right in the fire in a few minutes, if we

can't get started with this motor! I don't see
what ails it."

"Can't we steer to one side, as it is?"

"No. We're right in a powerful current of air,
and steering won't do any good, until we have
some motion of our own. Turn the gasolene
lever on a little more, and see if you can get a
spark."

Tom did so, but no explosion resulted. The
twenty cylinders of the big engine remained mute.
The airship, meanwhile, was gathering speed,
sucked onward and downward as it was by the
draught from the fire. The roaring was plainer
now, and the crackling of the flames could be
heard plainly. The heat, too, grew more intense.

Frantically Tom and Mr. Sharp labored over
the motor. With the perverseness usual to gas
engines, it had refused to work at a critical moment.

"What shall I do?" cried Mr. Damon from his
position in the pilot house. "We seem to be
heading right for the midst of it?"

"Slant the elevation rudder," called Tom. "Send
the ship up. It will be cooler the higher we go.
Maybe we can float over it!"

"You'd better go out there," advised Mr. Sharp.
"I'll keep at this motor. Go up as high as you

can. Turn on more gas. That will elevate us, but maybe not quick enough. The gas doesn't generate well in great heat. I'm afraid we're in for it," he added grimly.

Tom sprang to relieve Mr. Damon. The heat was now intense. Nearer and nearer came the *Red Cloud* to the blazing forest, which seemed to cover several square miles. Great masses of smoke, with huge pieces of charred and blazing wood carried up by the great draught, circled around the ship. The *Red Cloud* was being pulled into the midst of the fire by the strong suction. Tom yanked over the elevation rudder, and the nose of the craft pointed upward. But it still moved downward, and, a moment later the travelers of the air felt as if they were over a fiery furnace.

CHAPTER XVII

"WANTED—FOR ROBBERY!"

CHOKING and gasping for breath, feeling as if they could not stand the intense heat more than a moment longer, the young inventor and his companions looked at each other. Death seemed ready to reach out and grasp them. The mass of heated air was so powerful that it swung and tossed the *Red Cloud* about as if it were a wisp of paper.

"We must do something!" cried Mr. Damon, beginning to take off his collar and vest. "I'm choking!"

"Lie down in the bottom of the car," suggested Mr. Sharp. "The smoke won't trouble you so much there."

The eccentric man, too startled, now, to use any of his "blessing" expressions, did so.

"Can't you start the motor?" asked Tom frantically, as he stuck to his post, with his hand on the steering wheel, the elevation lever jammed back as far as it would go.

"I've done my best," answered the balloonist, gasping as he swallowed some smoke. "I'm afraid —afraid it's all up with us. We should have steered clear of this from the first. My, how it roars!"

The crackling and snapping of the flames below them, as they fed on the dry wood, which no rain had wet for weeks, was like the rush of some great cataract. Up swirled the dark smoke-clouds, growing hotter and hotter all the while as the craft came nearer and nearer to the center of the conflagration.

"We must rise higher!" cried Tom. "It's our only chance. Turn on the gas machine full power, and fill the container. That will carry us up!"

"Yes, it's our only hope," muttered Mr. Sharp. "We must go up, but the trouble is the gas doesn't generate so fast when there's too much heat. We're bound to have to stay over this fiery pit for some time yet."

"We're going up a little!" spoke Tom hopefully, as he glanced at a gauge near him. "We're fifteen hundred feet now, and we were only twelve a while ago."

"Good! Keep the elevation rudder as it is, and I'll see what I can do with the gas," advised the balloonist. "It's our only hope," and he hurried into the engine room, which, like the other parts of the cabin, was now murky with choking vapor and soot.

Suddenly the elevation gauge showed that they were falling. The airship was going down.

"What's the matter?" called Mr. Damon, from the cabin floor.

"I don't know," answered Tom, "unless the rudder has broken."

He peered through the haze. No, the big elevation rudder was still in place, but it seemed to have no effect on the ship.

"It's a down draught!" cried Mr. Sharp. "We're being sucked down. It won't last but a few seconds. I've been in 'em before."

He seemed to have guessed rightly, for, the next instant the airship was shooting upward again, and relief came to the aeronauts, though it was not much, for the heat was almost unbearable, and they had taken off nearly all their clothing.

"Lighten ship!" sung out Mr. Sharp. "Toss over all the things you think we can spare, Tom. Some of the cases of provisions! We can get more—if we need 'em. We must rise, and the gas isn't generating fast enough!"

There was no need for the young inventor at the steering wheel now, for the craft simply could not be guided. It was swirled about, now this way, now that, by the currents of heated air. At times it would rise a considerable distance, only to be pulled down again, and, just before Tom began to toss overboard some boxes of food, it seemed that the end had come, for the craft went down so low that the upward leaping tongues of flame almost reached the lower frame.

"I'll help you," gasped Mr. Damon, and while he and Tom tossed from the cabin windows some of their stores, Mr. Sharp was frantically endeavoring to make the gas generate faster.

It was slow work, but with the lightening of the ship their situation improved. Slowly, so slowly that it seemed an age, the elevation pointer went higher and higher on the dial.

"Sixteen hundred feet!" sung out Tom, pausing for a look at the gauge. "That's the best yet!"

The heat was felt less, now, and every minute was improving their situation. Slowly the hand moved. The gas was being made in larger quantities now that the heat was less. Ten minutes more of agony, and their danger was over. They were still above the burning area, but sufficiently high so that only stray wisps of smoke enveloped them.

"Whew! But that was the worst ever!" cried Tom, as he sank exhausted on a bench, and wiped his perspiring face. "We sure were in a bad way!"

"I should say so," agreed Mr. Sharp. "And if we don't get a breeze we may have to stay here for some time."

"Why, can't you get that motor to work yet?" asked Mr. Damon. "Bless my gaiters, but I'm all in, as the boys say."

"I'll have another try at the machine now," replied Mr. Sharp. "Probably it will work now, after we're out of danger without the aid of it."

His guess proved correct, for, in a few minutes, with the aid of Tom, the motor started, the propellers revolved, and the *Red Cloud* was sent swiftly out of the fire zone.

"Now we'd better take account of ourselves, our provisions, and the ship," said Mr. Sharp, when they had flown about twenty miles, and were much refreshed by the cooler atmosphere. "I don't believe the craft is damaged any, except some of the braces may be warped by the heat. As for the provisions, you threw over a lot; didn't you, Tom?"

"Well, I had to."

"Yes, I guess you did. Well, we'll make a landing."

"Do you think it will be safe?" asked Mr.

Damon anxiously. "We might be fired upon again."

"Oh, there's no danger of that. But I'll take precautions. I don't want a big crowd around when we come down, so we'll pick out a secluded place and land just at dusk. Then in the morning we can look over the ship, and go to the nearest town to buy provisions. After that we can continue our journey, and we'll steer clear of forest fires after this."

"And people who shoot at us," added Mr. Damon.

"Yes. I wish I knew what that was done for," and once again came that puzzled look to the face of the balloonist.

The airship gently descended that evening in a large level field, a good landing being made. Just before the descent Tom took an observation and located, about two miles from the spot they selected for an "anchorage," a good-sized village.

"We can get provisions there," he announced.

"Yes, but we must not let it be known what they are for," said Mr. Sharp, "or we'll have the whole population out here. I think this will be a good plan: Tom, you and Mr. Damon go into town and buy the things we need. I'll stay here with the airship, and look it all over. You can arrange to have the stuff carted out here in the morning, and left at a point say about a quarter of a mile away. Then we can carry it to the ship. In that way no one will discover us, and we'll not be bothered with curiosity-seekers."

This was voted a good idea, and, when the landing had been made, and a hasty examination showed that the ship had suffered no great damage from the passage over the fire, the young inventor and Mr. Damon started off.

They soon found a good road, leading to town, and tramped along it in the early evening. The few persons they met paid little attention to them, save to bow in a friendly fashion, and, occasionally wish them good evening.

"I wonder where we are?" asked Tom, as they hurried along.

"In some southern town, to judge by the voices of the people, and the number of colored individuals we've met," answered Mr. Damon.

"Let's ask," suggested Tom.

"No, if you do they'll know we're strangers, and they may ask a lot of questions."

"Oh, I guess if it's a small place they'll know we're strangers soon enough," commented Tom. "But when we get to the village itself we can read the name on the store windows."

A few minutes later found them in the midst

of a typical southern town. It was Berneau, North Carolina, according to the signs, they saw.

"Here's a restaurant," called Tom, as they passed a neat-appearing one. "Let's go inside and get some supper before we buy our supplies."

"Good!" exclaimed Mr. Damon. "Bless my flapjacks, but I am beginning to feel hungry."

The eating place was a good one, and Tom's predictions about their being taken for strangers was verified, for, no sooner had they given their orders than the pretty, white girl, who waited on the table remarked:

"Ah reckon yo' all are from th' no'th; aren't yo'?"

She smiled, as she spoke, and Tom smiled back as he acknowledged it.

"Have you a paper—a newspaper I could look at?" he asked.

"Ah guess Ah can find one," went on the girl. "Ah reckon yo' all are from N' York. N' Yorkers are so desperant bent on readin' th' news." Her tones were almost like those of a colored person.

"Yes, we're from a part of New York," was Tom's reply.

When a newspaper was brought to him, after they had nearly finished their meal, the young inventor rapidly scanned the pages. Something on the front sheet, under a heading of big, black type caught his eye. He started as he read it:

WANTED FOR ROBBERY!

BANK LOOTERS ESCAPE IN RED AIRSHIP—FIRED AT BUT DISAPPEAR

"Great Jehosophat!" exclaimed Tom, in a low voice. "What on earth can this mean?"

"What?" inquired Mr. Damon. "Has anything happened?"

"Happened? I should say there had," was the answer. "Why, we're accused of having robbed the Shopton Bank of seventy-five thousand dollars the night before we left, and to have taken it away in the *Red Cloud*. There's a general alarm out for us! Why this is awful!"

"It's preposterous!" burst out Mr. Damon. "I'l have my lawyers sue this paper. Bless my stocks and bonds, I——!"

"Hush! Not so loud," cautioned Tom, for the pretty waitress was watching them curiously. "Here, read this, and then we'll decide what to do. But one thing is certain, we must go back to Shopton at once to clear ourselves of this accusation."

"Ha!" murmured Mr. Damon, as he read the article rapidly. "Now I know why they fired at us. They hoped to bring us down, capture us and get the five thousand dollars reward!"

CHAPTER XVIII

BACK FOR VINDICATION

Tom glanced around the restaurant. There were few persons in it save himself and Mr. Damon. The pretty waitress was still regarding the two curiously.

"We ought to take that paper along with us, to show to Mr. Sharp," said Tom, in a low voice to his friend. "I haven't had time to take it all in myself, yet. Let's go. I've had enough to eat; haven't you?"

"Yes. My appetite is gone now."

As they arose, to pay their checks the girl advanced.

"Can you tell me where I can get a copy of this paper?" asked Tom, as he laid down a generous tip on the table, for the girl. Her eyes opened rather wide.

"Yo' all are fo'gettin' some of yo' money." she said, in her broad, southern tones. Tom thought her the prettiest girl he ever seen, excepting Mary Nestor.

"Oh, that's for you," replied the young inventor. "It's a tip. Aren't you in the habit of getting them down here?"

"Not very often. Thank yo' all. But what did yo' all ask about that paper?"

"I asked where I could get a copy of it. There is something in it that interests me."

"Yes, an' Ah reckon Ah knows what it is," exclaimed the girl. "It's about that airship with th' robbers in it!"

"How do you know?" inquired Tom quickly, and he tried to seem cool, though he felt the hot blood mounting to his cheeks.

"Oh, Ah saw yo' all readin' it. Everybody down heah is crazy about it. We all think th' ship is comin' down this way, 'cause it says th' robbers was intendin' to start south befo' they robbed th' bank. Ah wish Ah could collect thet five thousand dollars. If Ah could see that airship, I wouldn't work no mo' in this eatin' place. What do yo' all reckon thet airship looks like?" and the girl gazed intently at Tom and Mr. Damon.

"Why, bless my—" began the eccentric man, but Tom broke in hurriedly:

"Oh, I guess it looks like most any other airship," for he feared that if his companion used any of his odd expressions he might be recognized, since our hero had not had time to read the article in the paper through, and was not sure whether or not a description of himself, Mr. Damon and Mr. Sharp was given.

"Well, Ah suah wish I could collect thet reward," went on the girl. "Everybody is on th' lookout. Yo' all ain't see th' airship; have yo' all?"

"Where can we get a paper like this?" asked Tom, again, not wanting to answer such a leading question.

"Why, yo' all is suah welcome to that one," was the reply. "Ah guess Ah can affo'd to give it to yo' all, after th' generous way yo' all behaved to me. Take it, an' welcome. But are yo' all suah yo' are done eatin'? Yo' all left lots."

"Oh, we had enough," replied Tom hurriedly. His sole aim now was to get away—to consult with Mr. Sharp, and he needed the paper to learn further details of the astonishing news. He and his friends accused of looting the bank, and taking away seventy-five thousand dollars in the airship! It was incredible! A reward of five thousand dollars offered for their capture! They might be arrested any minute, yet they could not go on without buying some provisions. What were they to do?

Once outside the restaurant, Mr. Damon and Tom walked swiftly on. They came to a corner where there was a street lamp, and there the young inventor paused to scan the paper again. It was the copy of a journal published in the nearby county seat, and contained quite a full account of the affair.

The story was told of how the bank had been broken into, the vault rifled and the money taken. The first clue, it said, was given by a youth named Andy Foger, who had seen a former acquaintance hanging around the bank with burglar tools. Tom recognized the description of himself as the "former acquaintence," but he could not understand the rest.

"Burglar tools? I wonder how Andy could say that?" he asked Mr. Damon.

"Wait until we get back, and we'll ask John Sharp," suggested his companion. "This is very strange. I am going to sue some one for spreading false reports about me! Bless my ledgers, why I have money on deposit in that bank! To think that I would rob it!"

"Poor dad!" murmured Tom. "This must be hard for him. But what about ordering food? Maybe if we buy any they will trail us, find the airship and capture it. I don't want to be arrested, even if I am innocent, and I certainly don't want the airship to fall into the hands of the police. They might damage it."

"We must go see Mr. Sharp," declared Mr. Damon, and back to where the *Red Cloud* was concealed they went.

To say that the balloonist was astonished is putting it mildly. He was even more excited than was Mr. Damon.

"Wait until I get hold of that Andy Foger!" he cried. "I'll make him sweat for this! I see he's already laid claim to the reward," he added, reading further along in the article. "He thinks he has put the police on our trail."

"So he seems to have done," added Tom. "The whole country has been notified to look out for us," the paper says. "We're likely to be fired upon whenever we pass over a city or a town."

"Then we'll have to avoid them," declared the balloonist.

"But we must go back," declared Tom.

"Of course. Back to be vindicated. We'll have to give up our trip. My, my! But this is a surprise!"

"I don't see what makes Andy say he saw me with burglar tools," commented Tom with a puzzled air.

Mr. Sharp thought for a moment. Then he exclaimed:

"It was that bag of tools I sent you after—the long wrenches, the pliers, and the brace and bits. You——"

"Of course!" cried Tom. "I remember now. The bag dropped and opened, and Andy and Sam saw the tools. But the idea of taking them for burglar tools!"

"Well, I suppose the burglars, whoever they were, did use tools similar to those to break open the vault," put in Mr. Damon. "Andy probably thought he was a smart lad to put the police on our track."

"I'll put him on the track, when I return," declared Mr. Sharp. "Well, now, what's to be done?"

"We've got to have food," suggested Tom.

"Yes, but I think we can manage that. I've been looking over the ship, as best I could in the dark. It seems to be all right. We can start early in the morning without anyone around here knowing we paid their town a visit. You and Mr. Damon go back to town, Tom, and order some stuff. Have the man leave it by the roadside early to-morrow morning. Tell him it's for some travelers, who will stop and pick it up. Pay him well, and tell him to keep quiet, as it's

for a racing party. That's true enough. We're
going to race home to vindicate our reputations.
I think that will be all right."

"The man may get suspicious," said Mr.
Damon.

"I hope not," answered the balloonist. "We've
got to take a chance, anyhow."

The plan worked well, however, the store keeper
promising to have the supplies on hand at the
time and place mentioned. He winked as Tom
asked him to keep quiet about it.

"Oh, I know yo' automobile fellers," he said
with a laugh. "You want to get some grub on the
fly, so you won't have to stop, an' can beat th'
other fellow. I know you, fer I see them automobile goggles stickin' out of your pocket."

Tom and Mr. Damon each had a pair, to use
when the wind was strong, but the young inventor had forgotten about his. They now served
him a good turn, for they turned the thoughts of
the storekeeper into a new channel. The lad let
it go at that, and, paying for such things as he
and Mr. Damon could not carry, left the store.

The aeronauts passed an uneasy night. They
raised their ship high in the air, anchoring it by a
rope fast to a big tree, and they turned on no
lights, for they did not want to betray their position. They descended before it was yet daylight.

and a little later hurried to the place where the provisions were left. They found their supplies safely on hand, and, carrying them into the airship, prepared to turn back to Shopton.

As the ship rose high in the air a crowd of negro laborers passing through a distant field, saw it. At once they raised a commotion, shouting and pointing to the wonderful sight.

"We're discovered!" cried Tom.

"No matter," answered Mr. Sharp. "We'll soon be out of sight, and we'll fly high the rest of this trip."

Tom looked down on the fast disappearing little hamlet, and he thought of the pretty girl in the restaurant.

CHAPTER XIX

WRECKED

WITH her nose headed north, the *Red Cloud* swung along through the air. Those on board were thinking of many things, but chief among them was the unjust accusation that had been made against them, by an irresponsible boy—the red-haired Andy Foger. They read the account in the paper again, seeking to learn from it new things at each perusal.

"It's just a lot of circumstantial evidence—that's what it is," said Tom. "I admit it might look suspicious to anyone who didn't know us, but Andy Foger has certainly done the most mischief by his conclusions. Burglar tools! The idea!"

"I think I shall sue the bank for damages," declared Mr. Damon. "They have injured my reputation by making this accusation against me. Anyhow, I'll certainly never do any more business with them, and I'll withdraw my ten thousand dollars deposit, as soon as we get back."

"Mr. Sharp doesn't seem to be accused of doing anything at all," remarked Tom, reading the article for perhaps the tenth time.

"Oh, I guess I'm a sort of general all-around bad man, who helped you burglars to escape with the booty," answered the balloonist, with a laugh. "I expect to be arrested along with you two."

"But must we be arrested?" inquired Tom anxiously. "I don't like that idea at all. We haven't done anything."

"This is my plan," went on Mr. Sharp. "We'll get back to Shopton as quickly as we can. We'll arrive at night, so no one will see us, and, leaving the airship in some secluded spot, we'll go to the police and explain matters. We can easily prove that we had nothing to do with the robbery. Why we were all home the night it happened! Mr. Swift, Mr. Jackson and Mrs. Baggert can testify to that."

"Yes," agreed Mr. Damon. "I guess they can. Bless my bank book, but that seems a good plan. We'll follow it."

Proceeding on the plan which they had decided was the best one, the *Red Cloud* was sent high into the air. So high up was it that, at times, it was above the clouds. Though this caused some little discomfort at first, especially to Mr. Damon, he soon became used to it, as did the others. And it had the advantage of concealing them from the persons below who might be on the lookout.

"For we don't want to be shot at again," explained Mr. Sharp. "It isn't altogether healthy, and not very safe. If we keep high up they can't see us; much less shoot at us. They'll take us for some big bird. Then, too, we can go faster."

"I suppose there will be another alarm sent out, from those negroes having sighted us," ventured Tom.

"Oh, yes, but those colored fellows were so excited they may describe us as having horns, hoofs and a tail, and their story may not be believed. I'm not worrying about them. My chief concern is to drive the *Red Cloud* for all she is worth. I want to explain some things back there in Shopton."

As if repenting of the way it had misbehaved over the forest fire, the airship was now swinging along at a rapid rate. Seated in the cabin the travelers would have really enjoyed the return trip had it not been for the accusation hanging over them. The weather was fine and clear, and as they skimmed along, now and then coming out from the clouds, they caught glimpses below them of the earth above which they were traveling. They had a general idea of their location, from knowing the town where the paper had given

them such astounding news, and it was easy to
calculate their rate of progress.

After running about a hundred miles or so, at
high speed Mr. Sharp found it necessary to slow
down the motor, as some of the new bearings
were heating. Still this gave them no alarm, as
they were making good time. They came to a
stop that night, and calculated that by the next
evening, or two at the latest, they would be back
in Shopton. But they did not calculate on an accident.

One of the cylinders on the big motor cracked,
as they started up next morning, and for some
hours they had to hang in the air, suspended by
the gas in the container, while Mr. Sharp and
Tom took out the damaged part, and put in a
spare one, the cylinders being cast separately. It
was dusk when they finished, and too late to
start up, so they remained about in the same
place until the next day.

Morning dawned with a hot humidness, unusual
at that time of the year, but partly accounted
for by the fact that they were still within the
influence of the southern climate. With a whizz
the big propellers were set in motion, and, with
Tom at the wheel, the ship being about three miles
in the air, to which height it had risen after the
repairs were made, the journey was recommenced.

"It's cooler up here than down below," re-marked Tom, as he shifted the wheel and rudder a bit, in response to a gust of wind, that heeled the craft over.

"Yes, I think we're going to have a storm," remarked Mr. Sharp, eyeing the clouds with a professional air. "We may run ahead of it, or right into it. We'll go down a bit, toward night, when there's less danger of being shot."

So far, on their return trip, they had not been low enough, in the day time, to be in any danger from persons who hoped to earn the five thousand dollars reward.

The afternoon passed quickly, and it got dark early. There was a curious hum to the wind, and, hearing it, Mr. Sharp began to go about the ship, seeing that everything was fast and taut.

"We're going to have a blow," he remarked, "and a heavy one, too. We'll have to make every-thing snug, and be ready to go up or down, as the case calls for."

"Up or down?" inquired Mr. Damon.

"Yes. By rising we may escape the blow, or, by going below the strata of agitated air, we may escape it."

"How about rain?"

"Well, you can get above rain, but you can't get below it, with the law of gravitation working as it does at present. How's the gas generator, Tom?"

"Seems to be all right," replied the young inventor, who had relinquished the wheel to the balloonist.

They ate an early supper, and, hardly had the dishes been put away, when from the west, where there was a low-flying bank of clouds, there came a mutter of thunder. A little later there was a dull, red illumination amid the rolling masses of vapor.

"There's the storm, and she's heading right this way," commented Mr. Sharp.

"Can't you avoid it?" asked Mr. Damon, anxiously.

"I could, if I knew how high it was, but I guess we'll wait and see how it looks as we get closer."

The airship was flying on, and the storm, driven by a mighty wind, was rushing to meet it. Already there was a sighing, moaning sound in the wire and wooden braces of the *Red Cloud*.

Suddenly there came such a blast that it heeled the ship over on her side.

"Shift the equilibrium rudders!" shouted Mr. Sharp to Tom, turning the wheel and various levers over to the lad. "I'm going to get more speed out of the motor!"

Tom acted just in time, and, after bobbing about like a cork on the water, the ship was righted, and sent forging ahead, under the influence of the propellers worked at top speed. Nor was this any too much, for it needed all the power of the big engine to even partially overcome the force of the wind that was blowing right against the *Red Cloud*. Of course they might have turned and flown before it, but they wanted to go north, not south—they wanted to face their accusers.

Then, after the first fury of the blast had spent itself, there came a deluge of rain, following a dazzling glare of lightning and a bursting crash of thunder.

In spite of the gale buffeting her, the airship was making good progress. The skill of Tom and the balloonist was never shown to better advantage. All around them the storm raged, but through it the craft kept on her way. Nothing could be seen but pelting sheets of water and swirling mist, yet onward the ship was driven.

The thunder was deafening, and the lightning nearly blinded them, until the electrics were switched on, flooding the cabin with radiance. Inside the car they were snug and dry, though the pitching of the craft was like that of a big liner in the trough of the ocean waves.

"Will she weather it, do you think?" called Mr.

Damon, in the ear of Mr. Sharp, shouting so as to be heard above the noise of the elements, and the hum of the motor.

The balloonist nodded.

"She's a good ship," he answered proudly.

Hardly had he spoken when there came a crash louder than any that had preceded, and the flash of rosy light that accompanied it seemed to set the whole heavens on fire. At the same time there was violent shock to the ship.

"We're hit! Struck by lightning!" yelled Tom.

"We're falling!" cried Mr. Damon an instant later.

Mr. Sharp looked at the elevation gauge. The hand was slowly swinging around. Down, down dropped the *Red Cloud*. She was being roughly treated by the storm.

"I'm afraid we're wrecked!" said the balloonist in a low voice, scarcely audible above the roar of the tempest. Following the great crash had come a comparatively light bombardment from the sky artillery.

"Use the gliding rudder, Tom," called Mr. Sharp, a moment later. "We may fall, but we'll land as easily as possible."

The wind, the rain, the lightning and thunder continued. Down, down sank the ship. Its fall was somewhat checked by the rudder Tom swung into place, and by setting the planes at a different angle. The motor had been stopped, and the propellers no longer revolved. In the confusion and darkness it was not safe to run ahead, with the danger of colliding with unseen objects on the earth.

They tried to peer from the windows, but could see nothing. A moment later, as they stared at each other with fear in their eyes, there came a shock. The ship trembled from end to end.

"We've landed!" cried Tom, as he yanked back on the levers. The airship came to a stop.

"Now to see where we are," said Mr. Sharp grimly, "and how badly we are wrecked."

CHAPTER XX

OUT of the cabin of the now stationary airship hurried the three travelers; out into the pelting rain, which was lashed into their faces by the strong wind. Tom was the first to emerge.

"We're on something solid!" he cried, stamping his feet. "A rock, I guess."

"Gracious, I hope we're not on a rock in the midst of a river!" exclaimed Mr. Damon. "Bless my soul, though! The water does seem to be running around my ankles."

"There's enough rain to make water run almost up to our necks," called Mr. Sharp, above the noise of the storm. "Tom, can you make out where we are?"

"Not exactly. Is the ship all right?"

"I can't see very well, but there appears to be a hole in the gas container. A big one, too, or we wouldn't have fallen so quickly."

The plight of the travelers of the air was anything but enviable. They were wet through, for it needed only a few minutes' exposure to the pelting storm to bring this about. They could not tell, in the midst of the darkness, where they were, and they almost feared to move for fear they might be on top of some rock or precipice, over which they might tumble if they took a false step.

"Let's get back inside the ship," proposed Mr. Damon. "It's warm and dry there, at all events. Bless my umbrella, I don't know when I've been so wet!"

"I'm not going in until I find out where we are," declared Tom. "Wait a minute, and I'll go in and get an electric flash lantern. That will show us," for the lightning had ceased with the great crash that seemed to have wrecked the *Red Cloud*. The rain still kept up, however, and there was a distant muttering of thunder, while it was so black that had not the lights in the cabin of the airship been faintly glowing they could hardly have found the craft had they moved ten feet away from it.

Tom soon returned with the portable electric lamp, operated by dry batteries. He flashed it on the surface of where they were standing, and uttered an exclamation.

"We're on a roof!" he cried.

"A roof?" repeated Mr. Damon.

"Yes; the roof of some large building, and what you thought was a river is the rain water running off it. See!"

The young inventor held the light down so his companions could observe the surface of that upon which the airship rested. There was no doubt of it. They were on top of a large building.

"If we're on a roof we must be in the midst of a city," objected Mr. Damon. "But I can't see any lights around, and we would see them if we were in a city, you know."

"Maybe the storm put the lights out of business," suggested Mr. Sharp. "That often occurs."

"I know one way we can find out for certain," went on Tom.

"How?"

"Start up our search lamp, and play it all around. We can't make sure how large this roof is in the dark, and it's risky trying to trace the edges by walking around."

"Yes, and it would be risky to start our search light going," objected Mr. Sharp. "People would see it, and there'd be a crowd up here in less than no time, storm or no storm. No, we've got to keep dark until I can see what's the matter. We must leave here before daylight."

"Suppose we can't?" asked Mr. Damon. "The crowds will be sure to see us then, anyhow."

"I am pretty sure we can get away," was the opinion of the balloonist. "Even if our gas container is so damaged that it will not sustain us, we are still an aeroplane, and this roof being flat will make a good place to start from. No, we can leave as soon as this storm lets up a little."

"Then I'm going to have a look and find out what sort of a building this is," declared Tom, and, while Mr. Sharp began a survey, as well as he could in the dark, of the airship, the young inventor proceeded cautiously to ascertain the extent of the roof.

The rain was not coming down quite so hard now, and Tom found it easier to see. Mr. Damon, finding he could do nothing to help, went back into the cabin, blessing himself and his various possessions at the queer predicament in which they found themselves.

Flashing his light every few seconds, Tom walked on until he came to one edge of the roof. It was very large, as he could judge by the time it took him to traverse it. There was a low parapet at the edge. He peered over, and an expanse of dark wall met his eyes.

"Must have come to one side," he reasoned.
"I want to get to the front. Then, maybe, I can
see a sign that will tell me what I want to know."

The lad turned to the left, and, presently came
to another parapet. It was higher, and orna-
mented with terra-cotta bricks. This, evidently,
was the front. As Tom peered over the edge of
the little raised ledge, there flashed out below him
hundreds of electric lights. The city illuminating
plant was being repaired. Then Tom saw flashing below him one of those large signs made of
incandescent lights. It was in front of the building, and as soon as our hero saw the words he
knew where the airship had landed. For what
he read, as he leaned over, was this:

MIDDLEVILLE ARCADE

Tom gave a cry.

"What's the matter?" called Mr. Sharp.

"I've discovered something," answered Tom,
hurrying up to his friend. "We're on top of the
Middleville Arcade building."

"What does that mean?"

"It means that we're not so very far from
home, and in the midst of a fairly large city.
But it means more than that."

"What?" demanded the balloonist, struck by

an air of excitement about the lad, for, as Tom stood in the subdued glow of the lights from one of the airship's cabin windows, all the others having been darkened as the storm slackened, his eyes shone brightly.

"This is the building where Anson Morse, one of the gang that robbed dad, once had an office," went on Tom eagerly. "That was brought out at the trial. And it's the place where they used to do some of their conspiring. Maybe some of the crowd are here now laying low."

"Well, if they are, we don't want anything to do with that gang," said Mr. Sharp. "We can't arrest them. Besides I've found out that our ship is all right, after all. We can proceed as soon as we like. There is only a small leak in the gas container. It was the generator machine that was put out of business by the lightning, and I've repaired it."

"I want to see if I can get any trace of the rascals. Maybe I could learn something from the janitor of the Arcade about them. The janitor is probably here."

"But why do you want to get any information about that gang?"

"Because," answered Tom, and, as Mr. Damon at that moment started to come from the cabin of the airship, the lad leaped forward and whis-

pered the remainder of the sentence into the ear
of the balloonist.

"You don't mean it!" exclaimed Mr. Sharp,
in a tense whisper. Tom nodded vigorously.

"But how can you enter the building?" asked
the other. "You can't drop over the edge."

"Down the scuttle," answered Tom. "There
must be one on the roof, for they have to come
up here at times. We can force the lock, if necessary. I want to enter the building and see where
Morse had his office."

"All right. Go ahead. I'll engage Mr. Damon
here so he won't follow you. It will be great
news for him. Go ahead."

Under pretense of wanting the help of the
eccentric man in completing the repairs he had
started, Mr. Sharp took Mr. Damon back into the
cabin. Tom, getting a big screw driver from
an outside tool-box, approached the scuttle on the
roof. He could see it looming up in the semi-
darkness, a sort of box, covering a stairway that
led down into the building. The door was locked,
but Tom forced it, and felt justified. A few minutes later, cautiously flashing his light, almost
like a burglar he thought, he was prowling around
the corridors of the office structure.

Was it deserted? That was what he wanted to
know. He knew the office Morse had formerly

occupied was two floors from the top. Tom
descended the staircase, trying to think up some
excuse to offer, in case he met the watchman or
janitor. But he encountered no one. As he reached
the floor where he knew Morse and his gang were
wont to assemble, he paused and listened. At
first he heard nothing, then, as the sound of the
storm became less he fancied he heard the murmur of voices.

"Suppose it should be some of them?" whispered Tom.

He went forward, pausing at almost every
other step to listen. The voices became louder.
Tom was now nearly at the office, where Morse
had once had his quarters. Now he could see it,
and his heart gave a great thump as he noticed
that the place was lighted. The lad could read
the name on the door. "Industrial Development
Company." That was the name of a fake concern
headed by Morse. As our hero looked he saw the
shadows of two men thrown on the ground glass.

"Some one's in there!" he whispered to himself. He could now hear the voices much plainer.
They came from the room, but the lad could not
distinguish them as belonging to any of the gang
with whom he had come in contact, and who had
escaped from jail.

The low murmur went on for several seconds.

The listener could make out no words. Suddenly the low, even mumble was broken. Some one cried out:

"There's got to be a divvy soon. There's no use letting Morse hold that whole seventy-five thousand any longer. I'm going to get what's coming to me, or——"

"Hush!" some one else cried. "Be quiet!"

"No, I won't! I want my share. I've waited long enough. If I don't get what's coming to me inside of a week, I'll go to Shagmon myself and make Morse whack up. I helped on the job, and I want my money!"

"Will you be quiet?" pleaded another, and, at that instant Tom heard some one's hand on the knob. The door opened a crack, letting out a pencil of light. The men were evidently coming out. The young inventor did not wait to hear more. He had a clue now, and, running on tiptoes, he made his way to the staircase and out of the scuttle on the roof.

CHAPTER XXI

ON THE TRAIL

"What's the matter, Tom?" asked Mr. Sharp, as the lad came hurrying along the roof, having taken the precaution to fasten the scuttle door as well as he could. "You seem excited."

"So would you, if you had heard what I did."

"What? You don't mean that some of the gang is down there?"

"Yes, and what's more I'm on the trail of the thieves who robbed the Shopton Bank of the seventy-five thousand dollars!"

"No! You don't mean it!"

"I certainly do."

"Then we'd better tell Mr. Damon. He's in the cabin."

"Of course I'll tell him. He's as much concerned as I am. He wants to be vindicated. Isn't it great luck, though?"

"But you haven't landed the men yet. Do you

mean to say that the same gang—the Happy
Harry crowd—robbed the bank?"

"I think so, from what I heard. But come inside and I'll tell you all about it."

"Suppose we start the ship first? It's ready
to run. There wasn't as much the matter with it
as I feared. The storm is over now, and we'll
be safer up in the air than on this roof. Did you
get all the information you could?"

"All I dared to. The men were coming out, so
I had to run. They were quarreling, and when
that happens among thieves——"

"Why honest men get their dues, everyone
knows that proverb," interrupted Mr. Damon,
again emerging from the cabin. "But bless my
quotation marks, I should think you'd have something better to do than stand there talking
proverbs."

"We have," replied Mr. Sharp quickly. "We're
going to start the ship, and then we have some
news for you. Tom, you take the steering wheel,
and I'll start the gas machine. We'll rise to some
distance before starting the propellers, and then
we won't create any excitement."

"But what news are you going to tell me?"
asked Mr. Damon. "Bless my very existence, but
you get me all excited, and then you won't gratify
my curiosity."

"In a little while we will," responded Mr. Sharp. Lively now, Tom. Some one may see this airship on top of the building, as it's getting so much lighter now, after the storm."

The outburst of the elements was almost over and Tom taking another look over the edge of the roof, could see persons moving about in the street below. The storm clouds were passing and a faint haze showed where a moon would soon make its appearance, thus disclosing the craft so oddly perched upon the roof. There was need of haste.

Fortunately the *Red Cloud* could be sent aloft without the use of the propellers, for the gas would serve to lift her. It had been found that lightning had struck the big, red aluminum container, but the shock had been a comparatively slight one, and, as the tank was insulated from the rest of the ship no danger resulted to the occupants. A rent was made in two or three of the gas compartments, but the others remained intact, and, when an increased pressure of the vapor was used the ship was almost as bouyant as before.

Into the cabin the three travelers hurried, dripping water at every step, for there was no time to change clothes. Then, with Tom and Mr. Sharp managing the machinery, the craft slowly rose. It was well that they had started for, when a few hundred feet above the roof, the moon suddenly shone from behind a bank of clouds and would most certainly have revealed their position to persons in the street. As it was several were attracted by the sight of some great object in the air. They called the attention of others to it, but, by the time glasses and telescopes had been brought to bear, the *Red Cloud* was far away.

"Dry clothes now, some hot drinks, and then Tom will tell us his secret," remarked Mr. Sharp, and, with the great ship swaying high above the city of Middleville Tom told what he had heard in the offiice building.

"They are the thieves who looted the bank, and caused us to be unjustly accused," he finished. "If we can capture them we'll get the reward, and turn a neat trick on Andy Foger and his cronies."

"But how can you capture them?" asked Mr. Damon. "You don't know where they are."

"Perhaps not where Morse and the men who have the money are. But I have a plan. It's this: We'll go to some quiet place, leave the airship, and then inform the authorities of our suspicions. They can come here and arrest the men who still seem to be hanging out in Morse's office. Then we can get on the trail of this Shagmon, who seems to be the person in authority this time, though I never heard of him before.

He seems to have the money, according to what one of the men in the office said, and he's the man we want."

"Shagmon!" exclaimed Mr. Damon.

"Yes, Shagmon. The fellow I heard talking said he'd go to Shagmon and make Morse whack up. Shagmon may be the real head of the gang."

"Ha! I have it!" cried Mr. Damon suddenly. "I wonder I didn't think of it before. Shagmon is the headquarters, not the head of the gang!"

"What do you mean?" asked Tom, much excited.

"I mean that there's a town called Shagmon about fifty miles from here. That's what the fellow in the office meant. He is going to the town of Shagmon and make Morse whack up. That's where Morse is! That's where the gang is hiding! That's where the money is! Hurrah, Tom, we're on the trail!"

CHAPTER XXII

THE SHERIFF ON BOARD

THE announcement of Mr. Damon came as a great surprise to Tom and Mr. Sharp. They had supposed that the reference to Shagmon was to a person, and never dreamed that it was to a locality. But Mr. Damon's knowledge of geography stood them in good stead.

"Well, what's the first thing to do?" asked Tom, after a pause.

"The first thing would be to go to Shagmon, or close to it, I should say," remarked Mr. Sharp. "In what direction is it, Mr. Damon?"

"Northwest from where we were. It's a county seat, and that will suit our plans admirably, for we can call on the sheriff for help."

"That is if we locate the gang," put in Tom. "I fancy it will be no easy job, though. How are we going about it?"

"Let's first get to Shagmon," suggested the balloonist. "We'll select some quiet spot for a landing, and then talk matters over. We may stumble on the gang, just as you did, Tom, on the men in the office."

"No such good luck, I'm afraid."

"Well, I think we'll all be better for a little sleep," declared the eccentric man. "Bless my eyelids but I'm tired out."

As there was no necessity for standing watch, when the airship was so high up as to be almost invisible, they all turned in, and were soon sleeping soundly, though Tom had hard work at first to compose himself, for he was excited at the prospect of capturing the scoundrels, recovering the money for the bank, and clearing his good name, as well as those of his friends.

In the morning careful calculations were made to enable the travelers to tell when they had reached a point directly over the small city of Shagmon, and, with the skill of the veteran balloonist to aid them, this was accomplished. The airship was headed in the proper direction, and, about ten o'clock, having made out by using telescopes, that there was plenty of uninhabited land about the city, the craft was sent aloft again, out of a large crowd that had caught sight of it. For it was the intention of the travelers not to land until after dark, as they wanted to keep their arrival quiet. There were two reasons for this. One was that the whole country was eager to arrest them, to claim the reward offered by the bank, and they did not want this to happen. The other reason was that they wanted to go quietly into town, tell the sheriff their story, and enlist his aid.

All that day the *Red Cloud* consorted with the masses of fleecy vapor, several miles above the earth, a position being maintained, as nearly as could be judged by instruments, over a patch of woodland where Mr. Sharp had decided to land, as there were several large clearings in it. Back and forth above the clouds, out of sight, the air-ship drifted lazily to and fro; sometimes, when she got too far off her course being brought back to the right spot by means of the propellers.

It was tedious waiting, but they felt it was the only thing to do. Mr. Sharp and Tom busied themselves making adjustments to several parts of apparatus that needed it. Nothing could be done toward repairing the hole in the aluminum container until a shop or shed was reached, but the ship really did not need these repairs to enable it to be used. Mr. Damon was fretful, and "blessed" so many things during the course of the day that there seemed to be nothing left. Dinner and supper took up some time, really good meals being served by Tom, who was temporarily acting as cook. Then they anxiously waited for darkness, when they could descend.

"I hope the moon isn't too bright," remarked Mr. Sharp, as he went carefully over the motor once more, for he did not want it to balk again. "If it shines too much it will discover us."

"But a little light would be a fine thing, and show us a good place to land," argued Tom.

Fortune seemed to favor the adventurers. There was a hazy light from the moon, which was covered by swiftly moving dark clouds, now and then, a most effective screen for the airship, as its great, moving shape, viewed from the earth, resembled nothing so much as one of the clouds.

They made a good landing in a little forest glade, the craft, under the skillful guidance of Mr. Sharp and Tom, coming down nicely.

"Now for a trip to town to notify the sheriff," said Mr. Sharp. "Tom, I think you had better go alone. You can explain matters, and Mr. Damon and I will remain here until you come back. I should say what you had best do, would be to get the sheriff to help you locate the gang of bank robbers. They're in this vicinity and he ought to be able, with his deputies, to find them."

"I'll ask him," replied Tom, as he set off.

It was rather a lonely walk into the city, from the woods where the airship had landed, but Tom did not mind it, and, reaching Shagmon, he inquired his way to the home of the sheriff, for it was long after office hours. He heard, as he walked along the streets, many persons discussing the appearance of the airship that morning, and he was glad they had planned to land after dark, for more than one citizen was regretting that he had not had a chance to get the five thousand dollars reward offered for the arrest of the passengers in the *Red Cloud*.

Tom found the sheriff, Mr. Durkin by name, a genial personage. At the mention of the airship the official grew somewhat excited.

"Are you one of the fellows that looted the bank?" he inquired, when Tom told him how he and his friends had arrived at Shagmon.

The young inventor denied the impeachment, and told his story. He ended up with a request for the sheriff's aid, at the same time asking if the officer knew where such a gang as the Happy Harry one might be in hiding.

"You've come just at the right time, young man," was the answer of Sheriff Durkin, when he was assured of the honesty of Tom's statements. "I've been on the point, for the last week, of raiding a camp of men, who have settled at a disused summer resort about ten miles from here. I think they're running a gambling game, but I haven't been able to get any evidence, and every time I sent out a posse some one warns the men, and we can find nothing wrong. I believe these men are the very ones you want. If we could only get to them without their suspecting it, I think I'd have them right."

"We can do that, Sheriff."

"How?"

"Go in our airship! You come with us, and we'll put you right over their camp, where you can drop down on their heads."

"Good land, I never rode in an automobile even, let alone an airship!" went on the officer. "I'd be scared out of my wits, and so would my deputies."

"Send the deputies on ahead," suggested Tom.

The sheriff hesitated. Then he slapped his thigh with his big hand.

"By golly! I'll go you!" he declared. "I'll try capturing criminals in an airship for the first, time in my life! Lead the way, young man!"

An hour later Sheriff Durkin was aboard the *Red Cloud,* and plans were being talked of for the capture of the bank robbers, or at least for raiding the camp where the men were supposed to be.

CHAPTER XXIII

ON TO THE CAMP

"WELL, you sure have got a fine craft here," remarked Sheriff Durkin, as he looked over the airship after Tom and his friends had told of their voyage. "It will be quite up-to-date to raid a gang of bank robbers in a flying machine, but I guess it will be the only way we can catch those fellows. Now I'll go back to town, and the first thing in the morning I'll round-up my posse and start it off. The men can surround the camp, and lay quiet until we arrive in this ship. Then, when we descend on the heads of the scoundrels, right out of the sky, so to speak, my men can close in, and bag them all."

"That's a good plan," commented Mr. Sharp, "but are you sure these are the men we want? It's pretty vague, I think, but of course the clue Tom got is pretty slim; merely the name Shagmon."

"Well, this is Shagmon," went on the sheriff,

"and, as I told your young friend, I've been trying for some time to bag the men at the summer camp. They number quite a few, and if they don't do anything worse, they run a gambling game there. I'm pretty sure, if the bank robbers are in this vicinity, they're in that camp. Of course all the men there may not have been engaged in looting the vault, and they may not all know of it, but it won't do any harm to round-up the whole bunch."

After a tour of the craft, and waiting to take a little refreshment with his new friends, the sheriff left, promising to come as early on the morrow as possible.

"Let's go to bed," suggested Mr. Sharp, after a bit. "We've got hard work ahead of us to-morrow."

They were up early, and, in the seclusion of the little glade in the woods, Tom and Mr. Sharp went over every part of the airship.

The sheriff arrived about nine o'clock, and announced that he had started off through the woods, to surround the camp, twenty-five men.

"They'll be there at noon," Mr. Durkin said, "and will close in when I give the signal, which will be two shots fired. I heard just before I came here that there are some new arrivals at the camp."

"Maybe those are the men I overheard talking in the office building," suggested Tom. "They probably came to get their share. Well, we must swoop down on them before they have time to distribute the money."

"That's what!" agreed the county official. Mr. Durkin was even more impressed by the airship in the daytime than he had been at night. He examined every part, and when the time came to start, he was almost as unconcerned as any of the three travelers who had covered many hundreds of miles in the air.

"This is certainly great!" cried the sheriff, as the airship rose swiftly under the influence of the powerful gas.

As the craft went higher and higher his enthusiasm grew. He was not the least afraid, but then Sheriff Durkin was accounted a nervy individual under all circumstances.

"Lay her a little off to the left," the officer advised Tom who was at the steering wheel. "The main camp is right over there. How long before we will reach it?"

"We can get there in about fifteen minutes, if we run at top speed," answered the lad, his hand on the switch that controlled the motor. "Shall we?"

"No use burning up the air. Besides, my men

have hardly had time to surround the camp. It's in deep woods. If I were you I'd get right over it, and then rise up out of sight so they can't see you. Then, when it's noon you can go down, I'll fire the signal and the fun will commence—that is, fun for us, but not so much for those chaps, I fancy," and the sheriff smiled grimly.

The sheriff's plan was voted a good one, and, accordingly, the ship, after nearing a spot about over the camp, was sent a mile or two into the air, hovering as nearly as possible over one spot.

Shortly before twelve, the sheriff having seen to the weapons he brought with him, gave the signal to descend. Down shot the *Red Cloud* dropping swiftly when the gas was allowed to escape from the red container, and also urged toward the earth by the deflected rudder.

"Are you all ready?" cried the sheriff, looking at his watch.

"All ready," replied Mr. Sharp.

"Then here goes," went on the officer, drawing his revolver, and firing two shots in quick succession.

Two shots from the woods below answered him. Faster dropped the *Red Cloud* toward the camp of the criminals.

CHAPTER XXIV

THE RAID

"Look for a good place to land!" cried Mr. Sharp to Tom. "Any small, level place will do. Turn on the gas full power as soon as you feel the first contact, and then shut it off so as to hold her down. Then jump out and take a hand in the fight!"

"That's right," cried the sheriff. "Fight's the word! They're breaking from cover now," he added, as he looked over the side of the cabin, from one of the windows. "The rascals have taken the alarm!"

The airship was descending toward a little glade in the woods surrounding the old picnic ground. Men, mostly of the tramp sort, could be seen running to and fro.

"I hope my deputies close in promptly," murmured the sheriff. "There's a bigger bunch there than I counted on."

From the appearance of the gang rushing about

it seemed as if there were at least fifty of them. Some of the fellows caught sight of the airship, and, with yells, pointed upward.

Nearer and nearer to the earth settled the *Red Cloud*. The criminals in the camp were running wildly about. Several squads of them darted through the woods, only to come hurriedly back, where they called to their companions.

"Ha! My men are evidently on the job!" exclaimed the sheriff. "They are turning the rascals back!"

Some of the gang were so alarmed at the sight of the great airship settling down on their camp, that they could only stand and stare at it. Others were gathering sticks and stones, as if for resistance, and some could be seen to have weapons. Off to one side was a small hut, rather better than the rest of the tumbledown shacks in which the tramps lived. Tom noticed this, and saw several men gathered about it. One seemed familiar to the lad. He called the attention of Mr. Damon to the fellow.

"Do you know him?" asked Tom eagerly.

"Bless my very existence! If it isn't Anson Morse! One of the gang!" cried the eccentric man.

"That's what I thought," agreed Tom. "The bank robbers are here," he added, to the sheriff.

"If we only recover the money we'll be doing well," remarked Mr. Sharp.

Suddenly there came a shout from the fringe of woods surrounding the camp, and an instant later there burst from the bushes a number of men.

"My posse!" cried the sheriff. "We ought to be down now!"

The airship was a hundred feet above the ground, but Tom, opening wider the gas outlet, sent the craft more quickly down. Then, just as it touched the earth, he forced a mass of vapor into the container, making the ship buoyant so as to reduce the shock.

An instant later the ship was stationary.

Out leaped the sheriff.

"Give it to 'em, men!" he shouted.

With a yell his men responded, and fired a volley in the air.

"Come on, Tom!" called Mr. Sharp. "We'll make for the hut where you saw Morse."

"I'll come too! I'll come too!" cried Mr. Damon, rushing along as fast as he could, a seltzer bottle in either hand.

Tom's chief interest was to reach the men he suspected were the bank robbers. The lad dashed through the woods toward the hut near which he had seen Morse. He and Mr. Sharp reached it about the same time. As they came in front of it out dashed Happy Harry, the tramp. He was followed by Morse and the man named Featherton. The latter carried a black valise.

"Hey! Drop that!" shouted Mr. Sharp.

"Drop nothing!" yelled the man.

"Go on! Go on!" urged Morse. "Take to the woods! We'll deal with these fellows!"

"Oh, you will, eh?" shouted Tom, and remembering his football days he made a dive between Morse and Happy Harry for the man with the bag, which he guessed contained the stolen money. The lad made a good tackle, and grabbed Featherton about the legs. He went down in a heap, with Tom on top. Our hero was feeling about for the valise, when he felt a stunning blow on the back of his head. He turned over quickly to see Morse in the act of delivering a second kick. Tom grew faint, and dimly saw the leader of the gang reach down for the valise.

This gave our hero sudden energy. He was not going to lose everything, when it was just within his grasp. Conquering, by a strong effort, his feeling of dizziness, he scrambled to his feet, and made a grab for Morse. The latter fended him off, but Tom came savagely back at him, all his fighting blood up. The effects of the cowardly blow were passing off.

The lad managed to get one hand on the handle
of the bag.

"Let go!" cried Morse, and he dealt Tom a
blow in the face. It staggered the youth, but
he held on grimly, and raised his left hand and
arm as a guard. At the same time he endeavored
to twist the valise loose from Morse's hold. The
man raised his foot to kick Tom, but at that
moment there was a curious hissing sound, and a
stream of frothy liquid shot over the lad's head
right into the face of the man, blinding him.

"Ha! Take that! And more of it!" shouted
Mr. Damon, and a second stream of seltzer
squirted into the face of Morse.

With a yell of rage he let go his hold of the
satchel, and Tom staggered back with it. The
lad saw Mr. Damon rushing toward the now
disabled leader, playing both bottles of seltzer on
him. Then, when all the liquid was gone the
eccentric man began to beat Morse over the head
and shoulders with the heavy bottles until the
scoundrel begged for mercy.

Tom was congratulating himself on his success
in getting the bag when Happy Harry, the tramp,
rushed at him.

"I guess I'll take that!" he roared, and, wheeling Tom around, at the same time striking him

full in the face, the ugly man made a grab for the valise.

His hand had hardly touched it before he went down like a log, the sound of a powerful blow causing Tom to look up. He saw Mr. Sharp standing over the prostrate tramp, who had been cleanly knocked out.

"Are you all right, Tom?" asked the balloonist.

"Yes—trifle dizzy, that's all—I've got the money!"

"Are you sure?"

Tom opened the valise. A glance was enough to show that it was stuffed with bills.

Happy Harry showed signs of coming to, and Mr. Sharp, with a few turns of a rope he had brought along, soon secured him. Morse was too exhausted to fight more, for the seltzer entering his mouth and nose, had deprived him of breath, and he fell an easy prisoner to Mr. Damon.

Morse was soon tied up. The other members of the Happy Harry gang had escaped.

Meanwhile the sheriff and his men were having a fight with the crowd of tramps, but as the posse was determined and the criminals mostly of the class known as "hobos," the battle was not a very severe one. Several of the sheriff's men were slightly injured, however, and a few of the tramps escaped.

"A most successful raid," commented the sheriff, when quiet was restored, and a number of prisoners were lined up, all tied securely. "Did you get the money?"

"Almost all of it," answered Tom, who, now that Morse and Happy Harry were securely tied, had busied himself, with the aid of Mr. Sharp and Mr. Damon, in counting the bills. "Only about two thousand dollars are missing. I think the bank will be glad enough to charge that to profit and loss."

"I guess so," added the sheriff. "I'm certainly much obliged to you for the use of your airship. Otherwise the raid wouldn't have been so successful. Well, now we'll get the prisoners to jail."

It was necessary to hire rigs from nearby farmers to accomplish this. As for Morse and Happy Harry, they were placed in the airship, and, under guard of the sheriff and two deputies, were taken to the county seat. The criminals were too dazed over the rough treatment they had received, and over their sudden capture, to notice the fact of riding through the air to jail.

"Now for home!" cried Tom, when the prisoners had been disposed of. "Home to clear our names and take this money to the bank!"

"And receive the reward," added Mr. Sharp, with a smile. "Don't forget that!"

"Oh, yes, and I'll see that you get a share too, Mr. Durkin," went on Tom. "Only for your aid we never would have gotten these men and the money."

"Oh, I guess we're about even on that score," responded the official. "I'm glad to break up that gang."

The next morning Tom and his friends started for home in the *Red Cloud*.

They took with them evidence as to the guilt of the two men—Morse and Happy Harry. The men confessed that they and their pals had robbed the bank of Shopton, the night before Tom and his friends sailed on their trip. In fact that was the object for which the gang hung around Shopton. After securing their booty they had gone to the camp of the tramps at Shagmon, where they hid, hoping they would not be traced. But the words Tom had overheard had been their undoing. The men who arrived at the camp just before the raid were the same ones the young inventor heard talking in the office building. They had come to get their share of the loot, which Morse held, and with which he tried so desperately to get away. Tom's injuries were not serious and did not bother him after being treated by a physician.

CHAPTER XXV

ANDY GETS HIS REWARD

FLYING swiftly through the air the young inventor and his two companions were soon within sight of Shopton. As they approached the town from over the lake, and a patch of woods, they attracted no attention until they were near home, and the craft settled down easily in the yard of the Swift property.

That the aged inventor was glad to see his son back need not be said, and Mrs. Baggert's welcome was scarcely less warm than that of Mr. Swift. Mr. Sharp and Mr. Damon were also made to feel that their friends were glad to see them safe again.

"We must go at once and see Mr. Pendergast, the bank president," declared Mr. Swift. "We must take the money to him, and demand that he withdraw the offer of reward for your arrest."

"Yes," agreed Tom. "I guess the reward will go to some one besides Andy Foger."

There was considerable surprise on the part of the bank clerks when our hero, and his friends, walked in, carrying a heavy black bag. But they could only conjecture what was in the wind, for the party was immediately closeted with the president.

Mr. Pendergast was so startled that he hardly knew what to say when Tom, aided by Mr. Sharp, told his story. But the return of the money, with documents from Sheriff Durkin, certifying as to the arrest of Morse and Happy Harry, soon convinced him of the truth of the account.

"It's the most wonderful thing I ever heard," said the president.

"Well, what are you going to do about it?" asked Mr. Damon. "You have accused Tom and myself of being thieves, and——"

"I apologize—I apologize most humbly!" exclaimed Mr. Pendergast. "I also——"

"What about the reward?" went on Mr. Damon. "Bless my bank notes, I don't want any of it, for I have enough, but I think Tom and Mr. Sharp and the sheriff are entitled to it."

"Certainly," said the president, "certainly. It will be paid at once. I will call a meeting of the directors. In fact they are all in the bank now, save Mr. Foger, and I can reach him by telephone. If you will just rest yourselves in that room there

I will summon you before the board, when it convenes, and be most happy to pay over the five thousand dollars reward. It is the most wonderful thing I ever heard of—most wonderful!"

In a room adjoining that of the president, Tom, his father and Mr. Damon waited for the directors to meet. Mr. Foger could be heard entering a little later.

"What's this I hear, Pendergast?" he cried, rubbing his hands. "The bank robbers captured, eh? Well, that's good news. Of course we'll pay the reward. I always knew my boy was a smart lad. Five thousand dollars will be a tidy sum for him. Of course his chum, Sam Snedecker is entitled to some, but not much. So they've caught Tom Swift and that rascally Damon, eh? I always knew he was a scoundrel! Putting money in here as a blind!"

Mr. Damon heard, and shook his fist.

"I'll make him suffer for that," he whispered.

"Tom Swift arrested, eh?" went on Mr. Foger. "I always knew he was a bad egg. Who caught them? Where are they?"

"In the next room," replied Mr. Pendergast, who loved a joke almost as well as did Tom. "They may come out now," added the president, opening the door, and sending Ned Newton in to summon Tom, Mr. Swift and Mr. Damon, who filed out before the board of directors.

"Gentlemen," began the president, "I have the pleasure of presenting to you Mr. Thomas Swift, Mr. Barton Swift and Mr. Wakefield Damon. I also have the honor to announce that Mr. Thomas Swift and Mr. Damon have been instrumental in capturing the burglars who recently robbed our bank, and I am happy to add that young Mr. Swift and Mr. Wakefield Damon have, this morning, brought to me all but a small part of the money stolen from us. Which money they succeeded, after a desperate fight——"

"A fight partly with seltzer bottles," interrupted Mr. Damon proudly. "Don't forget them."

"Partly with seltzer bottles," conceded the president with a smile. "After a fight they succeeded in getting the money back. Here it is, and I now suggest that we pay the reward we promised."

"What? Reward? Pay them? The money back? Isn't my son to receive the five thousand dollars for informing as to the identity of the thief—isn't he?" demanded Mr. Foger, almost suffocating from his astonishment at the unexpected announcement.

"Hardly," answered Mr. Pendergast dryly. "Your son's information happened to be very wrong. The tools he saw Tom have in the bag were airship tools, not burglar's. And the same gang that once robbed Mr. Swift robbed our bank. Tom Swift captured them, and is entitled to the reward. It will be necessary for us directors to make up the sum, personally, and I, for one, am very glad to do so."

"So am I," came in a chorus from the others seated at the table.

"But—er—I understood that my son—" stammered Mr. Foger, who did not at all relish having to see his son lose the reward.

"It was all a mistake about your son," commented Mr. Pendergast. "Gentlemen, is it your desire that I write out a check for young Mr. Swift?"

They all voted in the affirmative, even Mr. Foger being obliged to do so, much against his wishes. He was a very much chagrined man, when the directors' meeting broke up. Word was sent at once, by telegraph, to all the cities where reward posters had been displayed, recalling the offer, and stating that Tom Swift and Mr. Damon were cleared. Mr. Sharp had never been really accused.

"Well, let's go home," suggested Tom when he had the five-thousand-dollar check in his pocket.

"I want another ride in the *Red Cloud* as soon as it's repaired."

"So do I!" declared Mr. Damon.

The eccentric man and Mr. Swift walked on ahead, and Tom strolled down toward the dock, for he thought he would take a short trip in his motor-boat.

He was near the lake, not having met many persons, when he saw a figure running up from the water. He knew who it was in an instant— Andy Foger. As for the bully, at the sight of Tom he hesitated, than came boldly on. Evidently he had not heard of our hero's arrival.

"Ha!" exclaimed the red-haired lad, "I've been looking for you. The police want you, Tom Swift."

"Oh, do they?" asked the young inventor gently.

"Yes; for robbery. I'm going to get the reward, too. You thought you were smart, but I saw those burglar tools in your valise. I sent the police after you. So you've come back, eh? I'm going to tell Chief Simonson. You wait."

"Yes," answered Tom, "I'll wait. So the police want me, do they?"

"That's what they do," snarled Andy. "I told you I'd get even with you, and I've done it."

"Well," burst out Tom, unable to longer contain

himself, as he thought of all he had suffered at the hands of the red-haired bully, "I said I'd get even with you, but I haven't done it yet. I'm going to now. Take off your coat, Andy. You and I are going to have a little argument."

"Don't you dare lay a finger on me!" blustered the squint-eyed one.

Tom peeled off his coat. Andy, who saw that he could not escape, rushed forward, and dealt the young inventor a blow on the chest. That was all Tom wanted, and the next instant he went at Andy hammer and tongs. The bully tried to fight, but he had no chance with his antagonist, who was righteously angry, and who made every blow tell. It was a sorry-looking Andy Foger who begged for mercy a little later.

Tom had no desire to administer more than a deserved reward to the bully, but perhaps he did add a little for interest. At any rate Andy thought so.

"You just wait!" he cried, as he limped off "I'll make you sorry for this."

"Oh, don't go to any trouble on my account," said Tom gently, as he put on his coat. But Andy did go to considerable trouble to be revenged on the young inventor, and whether he succeeded or not you may learn by reading the fourth book of this series, to be called "Tom Swift and His

Submarine Boat; or, Under the Ocean for Sunken Treasure," in which I shall relate the particulars of a voyage that was marvelous in the extreme.

Tom reached home in a very pleasant frame of mind that afternoon. Things had turned out much better than he thought they would. A few weeks later the two bank robbers, who were found guilty, were sentenced to long terms, but their companions were not captured. Tom sent Sheriff Durkin a share of the reward, and the lad invested his own share in bank stock, after giving some to Mr. Sharp. Mr. Damon refused to accept any. As for Mr. Swift, once he saw matters straightened out, and his son safe, he resumed his work on his prize submarine boat, his son helping him.

As for Tom, he alternated his spare time between trips in the airship and his motor-boat, and frequently a certain young lady from the Rocksmond Seminary was his companion. I think you know her name by this time. Now, for a while, we will take leave of Tom Swift and his friends, trusting to meet them again.

THE END

This Isn't All!

Would you like to know what became of the good friends you have made in this book?

Would you like to read other stories continuing their adventures and experiences, or other books quite as entertaining by the same author?

On the *reverse side* of the wrapper which comes with this book, you will find a wonderful list of stories which you can buy at the same store where you got this book.

Don't throw away the Wrapper

Use it as a handy catalog of the books you want some day to have. But in case you do mislay it, write to the Publishers for a complete catalog.

THE TOM SWIFT SERIES

By VICTOR APPLETON

Uniform Style of Binding. Individual Colored Wrappers.
Every Volume Complete in Itself.

Every boy possesses some form of inventive genius. Tom Swift
is a bright, ingenious boy and his inventions and adventures make
the most interesting kind of reading.

TOM SWIFT AND HIS MOTOR CYCLE
TOM SWIFT AND HIS MOTOR BOAT
TOM SWIFT AND HIS AIRSHIP
TOM SWIFT AND HIS SUBMARINE BOAT
TOM SWIFT AND HIS WIRELESS MESSAGE
TOM SWIFT AND HIS ELECTRIC RUNABOUT
TOM SWIFT AMONG THE DIAMOND MAKERS
TOM SWIFT IN THE CAVES OF ICE
TOM SWIFT AND HIS SKY RACER
TOM SWIFT AND HIS ELECTRIC RIFLE
TOM SWIFT IN THE CITY OF GOLD
TOM SWIFT AND HIS AIR GLIDER
TOM SWIFT IN CAPTIVITY
TOM SWIFT AND HIS WIZARD CAMERA
TOM SWIFT AND HIS GREAT SEARCHLIGHT
TOM SWIFT AND HIS GIANT CANNON
TOM SWIFT AND HIS PHOTO TELEPHONE
TOM SWIFT AND HIS AERIAL WARSHIP
TOM SWIFT AND HIS BIG TUNNEL
TOM SWIFT IN THE LAND OF WONDERS
TOM SWIFT AND HIS WAR TANK
TOM SWIFT AND HIS AIR SCOUT
TOM SWIFT AND HIS UNDERSEA SEARCH
TOM SWIFT AMONG THE FIRE FIGHTERS
TOM SWIFT AND HIS ELECTRIC LOCOMOTIVE
TOM SWIFT AND HIS FLYING BOAT
TOM SWIFT AND HIS GREAT OIL GUSHER
TOM SWIFT AND HIS CHEST OF SECRETS
TOM SWIFT AND HIS AIRLINE EXPRESS
TOM SWIFT CIRCLING THE GLOBE
TOM SWIFT AND HIS TALKING PICTURES
TOM SWIFT AND HIS HOUSE ON WHEELS
TOM SWIFT AND HIS BIG DIRIGIBLE

GROSSET & DUNLAP, *Publishers*, NEW YORK

WESTERN STORIES FOR BOYS

By JAMES CODY FERRIS

Individual Colored Wrappers and Illustrations by
WALTER S. ROGERS
Each Volume Complete in Itself.

Thrilling tales of the great west, told primarily for boys but which will be read by all who love mystery, rapid action, and adventures in the great open spaces.

The Manly Boys, Roy and Teddy, are the sons of an old ranchman, the owner of many thousands of heads of cattle. The lads know how to ride, how to shoot, and how to take care of themselves under any and all circumstances.

The cowboys of the X Bar X Ranch are real cowboys, on the job when required but full of fun and daring—a bunch any reader will be delighted to know.

THE X BAR X BOYS ON THE RANCH
THE X BAR X BOYS IN THUNDER CANYON
THE X BAR X BOYS ON WHIRLPOOL RIVER
THE X BAR X BOYS ON BIG BISON TRAIL
THE X BAR X BOYS AT THE ROUND-UP
THE X BAR X BOYS AT NUGGET CAMP
THE X BAR X BOYS AT RUSTLER'S GAP
THE X BAR X BOYS AT GRIZZLY PASS
THE X BAR X BOYS LOST IN THE ROCKIES

GROSSET & DUNLAP, Publishers, NEW YORK

THE HARDY BOY'S SERIES
By FRANKLIN W. DIXON

Individual Colored Wrappers and Text Illustrations by
WALTER S. ROGERS
Every Volume Complete in Itself.

THE HARDY BOYS are sons of a celebrated American detective, and during vacations and their off time from school they help their father by hunting down clues themselves.

THE TOWER TREASURE

A dying criminal confessed that his loot had been secreted "in the tower." It remained for the Hardy Boys to make an astonishing discovery that cleared up the mystery.

THE HOUSE ON THE CLIFF

The house had been vacant and was supposed to be haunted. Mr. Hardy started to investigate—and disappeared! An odd tale, with plenty of excitement.

THE SECRET OF THE OLD MILL

Counterfeit money was in circulation, and the limit was reached when Mrs. Hardy took some from a stranger. A tale full of thrills.

THE MISSING CHUMS

Two of the Hardy Boys' chums take a motor trip down the coast. They disappear and are almost rescued by their friends when all are captured. A thrilling story of adventure.

HUNTING FOR HIDDEN GOLD

Mr. Hardy is injured in tracing some stolen gold. A hunt by the boys leads to an abandoned mine, and there things start to happen. A western story all boys will enjoy.

THE SHORE ROAD MYSTERY

Automobiles were disappearing most mysteriously from the Shore Road. It remained for the Hardy Boys to solve the mystery.

THE SECRET OF THE CAVES

When the boys reached the caves they came unexpectedly upon a queer old hermit.

THE MYSTERY OF CABIN ISLAND

A story of queer adventures on a rockbound island.

GROSSET & DUNLAP, Publishers, NEW YORK